Dancing *with* Darkness

Dancing *with* Darkness

Life, Death and Hope in Afghanistan

Magsie Hamilton Little

First published in the United Kingdom in 2011
by Max Press, Little Books Ltd,
73 Campden Hill Towers, 112 Notting Hill Gate, London W11 3QP.

10 9 8 7 6 5 4 3 2 1

The Publishers are grateful to CPI Mackays for their generosity and
help in producing this book.

ISBN: 978 1 906251 43 7

Printed in the UK by CPI Mackays, Chatham ME5 8TD

For the children of Afghanistan,
the brightest lights in the darkest nights

In honour of Maryam

Remember Me

I will be with you in the grave
on the night you leave behind
your shop and your family.
When you hear my soft voice
echoing in your tomb,
you will realise
that you were never hidden from my eyes.
I am the pure awareness within your heart,
with you during joy and celebration,
suffering and despair.

On that strange and fateful night
you will hear a familiar voice
you'll be rescued from the fangs of snakes
and the searing sting of scorpions.
When the light of realisation dawns,
shouting and upheaval
will rise up from the graves.
The dust of ages will be stirred
by the cities of ecstasy,
by the banging of drums,
by the clamour of revolt!

Dead bodies will tear off their shrouds
and stuff their ears in fright.
What use are the senses and the ears
before the blast of that Trumpet?
Look and you will see my form
whether you are looking at yourself
or toward that noise and confusion.

Don't be blurry-eyed,
See me clearly,
See my beauty without the old eyes of delusion.

Don't mistake me for this human form.
The soul is not obscured by forms.
Even if it were wrapped in a hundred folds of felt
the rays of the soul's light
would still shine through.

Beat the drum,
Follow the minstrels of the city.
It's a day of renewal
when every young man
walks boldly on the path of love.

Had everyone sought God
Instead of crumbs and copper coins
They would not be sitting on the edge of the moat
in darkness and regret.

What kind of gossip-house
have you opened in our city?
Close your lips
and shine on the world
like loving sunlight.

Shine like the Sun of Tabriz rising in the East.
Shine like the star of victory.
Shine like the whole universe is yours!

Jalaluddin Rumi

Contents

Part Two: In a Spin

Part Three: Sore Feet

Author's note

When writing this book it was not my intention to re-tread the ground of familiar arguments about the political, diplomatic and military situation in Afghanistan. Mine was a personal experience and my intention was to observe rather than to sit in judgement. I need hardly stress that many differences of opinion co-exist with regard to Islam, the war in Afghanistan, Britain, America and the West, as well as issues such as the burka and the veiling of women.

Many Afghans maintain that the Dari spoken in Afghanistan is a purer and more archaic form of the Farsi spoken throughout Iran. It is certainly very different, both in the pronunciation and in the specific words used. There are also inevitable regional differences. With this in mind, I have referred throughout the text to the burka, because it is a commonly understood term, although anyone who has visited or lived in Afghanistan will be aware that Afghans themselves use the term *chaderi*. Similarly, Ramadan is always spoken of as Ramazan in Afghanistan, but I have used Ramadan.

Prologue

London, 7 July 2005. A crisp, bright day.

I glanced at my watch and then it happened.

Afterwards, it was hard to remember what came first. I think it was the noise of the blast that temporarily deafened me. My ears stopped ringing and my mind at last cleared. I looked around, picked up my bag and ran.

A cloud of smoke hovered then gradually dissipated. The bus was torn open, the side of it peeling like a ripped apart pomegranate. There was a blaze at the back. Pieces of debris lay everywhere, a thousand shafts of glass and a mess of twisted metal. Windows were shattered. Doors hung open. And the air was filled with a chemical odour.

From the thud of the blast came an eery sort of calm. A girl cried aloud, clutching her briefcase like an old childhood teddy bear. Faces turned ashen were palsied with bewilderment. Foreheads furrowed as people tended to the wounded.

One man lay alone and was heavily bleeding. I bent down to help but he'd already stopped breathing.

A policeman rushed over to steer me away.

'What can I?' The words came out fast, but my voice wouldn't work properly.

'It's time you went home, love. Leave the experts to deal with it.'

I turned slowly away and began walking. My mind had gone blank. My courage had faded. As I stepped from the square only one thing was haunting me. The man who had lain there had died in the road. And I hadn't been able to save him.

PART ONE

First Steps

Chapter 1

'The One Bitten by a Snake is Scared of a Long Rope'

مارگزیده از ریسمان دراز میترسد

I wandered my way home through the streets full of strangers. I bought a sandwich I couldn't eat and a coffee I couldn't drink. On the way small details seemed to connect – the glint of a ring, the sparkle of a paving stone, a ripple of sunlight in a puddle.

Inside the flat I slumped on a chair and kicked off my shoes. I made tea and let it stand until it was stone cold and yellow. As I picked up the telephone my fingers were trembling. I fumbled for a number and gave up. I lay down on the bed, pulled the covers around me and hid in the darkness.

I woke to find the duvet in a tangled heap. My limbs were contorted and one leg was numb. A wiggling of toes, and the pins and needles tingled. I drew back the curtains, and the sun streamed in, lighting the motes of dust floating like snowflakes. The phone rang and stopped. I was glad. They would call back later, whoever they were.

In the hallway, a pile of newspapers was blocking the door. I dragged them inside, spread them across the carpet and sat down in the middle. A sea of faces stared back at me from the pages, victims of the bomb blasts. I glanced around, seeking a distraction, but saw only the gathering mess, the out-of-control washing up, the vase of daisies dying in their cloudy flower water, the dust-laden bookshelves.

I didn't have to be a student to know there were conflicting beliefs within Islam, but I had always been clear in my mind as to who thought what. There was the tolerant form of Islam advocated by moderate Muslims who argued passionately that it was just a wilful minority who held that violence in the form of Islamic *jihad* was morally and religiously acceptable. Those moderates condemned the slaughter of innocents, as any rational human being would do, arguing that it was only the extremist Muslims who interpreted *jihad* as holy war.

The bombings had shown us the reality was more complicated and the mistrust between us was stronger than ever. As I ran through the arguments, the clarity faded. How deep was the hatred? How far did it extend? Was common ground to hope for, or was it always to lie beyond us? These were big questions, and perhaps in the end they were unanswerable.

I lay on the carpet, remembering. It had been several years since I had visited Iran to research a paper I had been preparing. A meeting had been arranged via a string of intermediaries. The interview was with a student at Tehran University. The student in question was a woman and she had been willing to talk so I would tell people. Her name was Fatima. At first it had been hard to equate the content of what Fatima said with her serene demeanour. She looked the epitome of an Eastern beauty, her dark eyes framed by long eyelashes. I had told her immediately she was too beautiful to die young.

As her words flooded back now, they horrified me. Fatima had told me she belonged to Zaytoon, a group that openly advertised in newspapers and on television for would-be martyrs. To be accepted, the volunteers had to be convinced of the legitimacy of *jihad*. Conviction in the rightness of their cause and methods was paramount. The response to the adverts had apparently been overwhelming, with people queuing in their thousands to sign up, all deeply religious and all highly educated, middle-class and holding well-paid jobs.

Zaytoon provided physical and ideological training for all would-be martyrs, it transpired, including courses on explosives, surveillance, how to hijack planes, and gather information on targets, as well as Arabic and English classes. Trainees were provided with night-vision goggles, sleeping-bags and waterproof clothing. Training was given on how to fire automatic rifles and throw hand grenades. Lectures on the Qur'an encouraged them to kill Americans and Israelis who, in Fatima's view, wanted to destroy Islam.

Once their basic training was complete, each potential martyr was allocated to a martyrdom cell consisting of a leader and two or three young men or women, and was given the title *al shaheed al-hay*, 'living martyr' or 'one who is waiting for martyrdom'. Often the cells then penetrated the West, where members were parachuted into jobs in security or travel companies, or, in the case of women, married in to the so-called enemy society network. Each cell was given a name from the Qur'an, and young would-be *jihadis* entered a more intense period of prayer. They would recite verses from the Qur'an associated with *jihad*, war and Allah's favours; they made out wills on paper, video and audiocassette. Most of their time was divided between prayer and fasting, she told me, and when their mission approached they would be in a constant state of prayer and devotion. The feeling then would be of happiness and relief. It was a great honour to be selected to die for Allah, and the human bomb was the surest method of hitting a target and guaranteeing loss of life. It was also cheap. All you needed were nails, gunpowder, a battery, a light switch, a short cable, mercury (from thermometers), acetone, and the cost of adapting a belt to carry pockets of explosives.

Fatima had related the events of the final day, how before they set out they would perform ritual ablutions, dress in freshly cleaned clothes, and attend prayer in at least one mosque. They would repeat the traditional Islamic prayer that was said before entering into battle, and pray for the forgiveness of sins and a blessing on the mission. A copy of the Qur'an placed in a pocket near the heart, they would set off.

Their words were full of piety. The cell leader would tell them, 'May Allah be with you. May he give you success so you enter paradise', to which they responded, '*Inshallah*, we will meet in paradise.' Before pressing the button they would give final thanks to God: '*Allahu akbar*, God is great. All praise to him.'

After a successful mission, grief mingled with joy for the bomber's family, and the sponsoring organisation sent a copy of the video to the media. Zaytoon took care of everything. They helped the families of the martyr after their death, giving them between $3,000 and $5,000 to pay debts and improve their standard of living, even to start new businesses. After a successful operation, aspiring martyrs re-enacted the operations using models of exploding cars and buses. Guests would gather at the house to offer their congratulations. Juices and sweets would be served and martyred *jihadis* sanctified, the most honoured people after the Prophet.

Jihad was subject to rigorous conditions. The detailed rules of combat banned harming civilians. Killing women, children and old people was forbidden under the sacred laws of holy war in Islam. In most Muslims eyes that was murder.

Fatima's view had been unwavering. 'This was war between East and West,' she had told me. 'In war innocent people get hurt.' The British, Americans and Israelis killed their women and children. They had no option but to fight back, she said. Her rage was not personal but reflected the outrage that every Muslim felt at the assault on their brother or sister. Western law and Western justice had been imposed on the Middle East for decades, resulting in defeat after defeat for her people and ultimately humiliation. Fundamentalism was military piety. It was a fight between truth and lies, between good and evil.

I had taken down my notes and flown directly back to London, never imagining that the implications of such thinking would touch my life so directly.

★ ☽ ★

It was another bleak, damp day. Summer had packed its bags and left, and the city felt gloomy. Nothing to see but streets and cars. Nothing to breathe but fumes and smoke.

Nothing to change the brooding mind or raise it up. Nothing to delete the monotony.

Life seemed to have clicked back in. People were still ordering their extra hot, half-decaf cappuccinos. Sales in Oxford Street offered goods at knock-down prices. Rain continued to drench summer picnics. Only the odd sign hinted at the events that had rocked us – a helicopter buzzing over Buckingham Palace, a policeman riding a bicycle.

At the School of Oriental and African Studies students loitered at the library steps, some with flowing beards, dressed in long white shirts and baggy trousers in the style of Maududi, the great Islamic reformer. Perhaps they believed those clothes would show their piety? They seemed oblivious of how closely they resembled Osama bin Laden. Dressed like that, they were asking for trouble.

As I walked down the street I desperately wanted to say something, but couldn't think how. Lost in my thoughts, I passed straight by a doorway. I hesitated, then went back. A low double knock at the bright brass knocker went unanswered. The door squeaked open and I peeped in cautiously, held by an urge to probe its mysteries. Inside the church there were no definable colours but the jewels of a stained-glass window, the altar bare, the air empty except for a pervading smell of must.

I sat on a pew, listening to the silence. It was in the silence God dwelt, they said, though what he was saying was beyond me. My failings were deafening, however, my inability to help at the scene of a bombing, my idealised view of Islam shattered, my father losing his fight against cancer. I had broken off an engagement to the disapproval of my friends. I had given up on happiness. And I had given up on love. It was only a short distance to giving up on myself. As the word sprang to mind, I dismissed it. Ten seconds later it came back. This time it stuck firm. I had already lived in a Middle Eastern country. I had trekked from Syria to Iran and spent my gap year in Palestine. The more I thought it through, the more it grew on me.

The word in my head was Afghanistan.

★ ☽ ★

In the hospital ward the air was stale. Daylight flooded through the drawn curtains, concealing the way to the open door. There was a waft of cabbage and a clattering of metal. In the room lay a bed and a chair by the window. Over the bed hung a sign, 'Nil by Mouth', with the words 'except for wine and chocolate' scribbled beneath in my father's hand. A figure, shrouded in green-striped pyjamas, sat hunched over a book.

At my approach the head lifted, the face illuminated, the book slammed shut. The sunken eyes sparkled as the patient croaked his greeting. I pecked the cheek, carefully avoiding the tubes that ran from the waist and throat, and sat uneasily on the end of the bed. My father looked terrible.

We motioned with hand gestures about the small things and tiptoed with ease around the big ones. In whispers he raved, recalling the scent of his favourite foods, the forbidden elixirs, fine wine and champagne. I worried it would upset him to speak of such things, but it only seemed to cheer him. Proust had been right, he mouthed gleefully, remembering all the tastes and the

7

textures, and like a bird his mind soared, though the saliva still dried in his ravaged mouth. We both knew well he would never eat again.

He shot me a look, as if a question wouldn't come. I handed him the notepad. Taking the pen in his shaky hand, he proceeded to write something. 'Nothing's wrong,' I mouthed, as if the absence of his voice was making my own fade.

I left him to rest. I walked to the entrance, my cheeks bone dry, as the tears fell inwards. How could I go and desert him now? And how could I abandon my mother?

★ ☽ ★

It was hard to believe it had been a week since the bomb blasts. I had left the city behind and all its stresses had evaporated. The tyres of my old two-seater juddered on the track. A duck waddled out in front of the bonnet. The duck stayed still, and I almost ran it over. My mind was elsewhere. That word was in my head again.

At the window of the house appeared a face lit with expectancy. 'I've been worried sick about you,' said my mother, rushing out to greet me. I kissed her back, and as she studied me closely there was no use either of us pretending.

Inside the house there were fresh flowers on the tables, old tea roses and hollyhocks. I breathed in the scents, the faded old rugs, the abstract paintings, the vestiges of my childhood. A cat wandered in, winked in the light, lithely spun herself on her back. Wriggling with abandon, she went floppy. I tickled under her chin and felt soft purrs, as if everything was well with the world.

An audience was gathering by the hearth in the drawing room. Aunts and uncles smiled worriedly. They took their places and the 'family discussion' began. It was less of a chat than a chorus of disapproval. Objections rose as if disembodied, like strangers echoing in the darkness in a Robbe-Grillet novel. There came a barrage of clichés.

'Tell me you are joking?'

'Afghanistan is a war zone!'

'Your parents only have you, you know . . . what if?'

'Running away never helped anyone . . . '

'Don't try changing the whole world...'

'Look, darling, we must face facts...'

'It's not that we don't trust you . . . '

'We know you are an adult . . . '

'Can't you go to Egypt?'

'Or Turkey?'

I sat dazed and remorseful, as a lone voice rose to defend me. 'I've never told you what to do,' said my mother. Her voice was a whisper because there was no need to shout when speaking the truth. She was aware I wasn't joking, but even she could not have guessed what no one could have known. I was about to set off on my very own suicide mission.

Some time later, I climbed into the car and drove back to London, having agreed a truce with my relatives. I changed my mind two, or maybe three, times during that journey and by the time I reached home had resolved it would be best to abandon the trip. In my head I called the whole thing off.

It was late when my mother phoned from the hospital.

She had told my father, and the message was unequivocal. He not only thought I should go, he insisted. It would give him something to live for.

★ ☽ ★

That message changed everything. I looked at the map and saw straight lines, translating the enormous distance into a few tiny centimetres. As I played down the space, the longing for distance seemed to grow in relation to the shortness on the page. It was a yearning for escape, for distance and for release.

I took a notepad from the drawer and made a list of things I should take. I read it again, screwed it up and discarded it. I reached into the wardrobe, grabbed all the contents in a pincer-like movement, and flung them on the bed in a heap. I stared at them blankly – the low, plunging necklines, the overly short party dresses, the diaphanous blouses. I had nothing to wear.

That afternoon Shepherd's Bush market came up trumps. I returned laden with trousers and loose-fitting tunics. There was little else to go in my rucksack apart from gifts, mainly sunglasses and cigarettes, not forgetting my industrial supply of blue Viagra capsules procured with surprising ease on the internet. I had been assured that this was the real clincher when it came to bribing Afghans juggling multiple wives. There remained just the matter of acquiring a visa, and there was one person I knew who could give trusty advice.

Friday was locals' day in Portobello Road. The weekend rush had yet to descend and the tourist quota was thin. At the hardware shop, Mr Noor stroked his straggly beard in greeting. His Afghan eyes sparkled. I was his best customer, after all, like all his other best customers. I grinned back, caught in the beam of his beautiful smile. As my eye wandered casually over the plastics and potato-peelers, he called over again. Suddenly I broke, and while I blurted it out, his eyes darted nervously.

Afterwards I felt much better, but the look on both our faces told him we needed to sit down. He gathered up some stools and patted them softly. As I perched on mine warily, he began railing. pondering the disadvantages with Faginesque hand-rubbing. The perch became a slump, and the slump became a heap. My legs uncrossed and my mouth hung open. The problems of Kabul were complex, he said. There were bombs every day, the officials were corrupt. The conditions were impossible. It was no place for a woman and it was no place for me.

Seeing the crestfallen look on my face he halted, scratched his chin and sighed. I was a good customer, and like all good businessmen he looked after his customers, he said, opening his jacket, taking out a pen and un-clicking it. He wrote with a flourish, a dash and a swirl, then handed over the paper to me. I took it and studied it. The content was an enigma, the ink barely legible, the address quite vague, though the words 'handful' and 'by the grace of God' leapt out like neon.

The person to whom it was addressed was a good man. He had the patience of a saint and the wit of a fox, he said, adding that with me he would need them. I thanked him for his kindness, and he nodded consolingly. It would only be a while before dysentery set in.

★ ☽ ★

I set off on foot, hugging the Serpentine. Light rebounded from the surface of the water and settled in a fine haze. A light rainfall had left a filmy coating on the ground, and the white path shimmered. There was no sound apart from the shallow patter of the water lapping the edges. I hastened my step and ran. It was further than I had anticipated, and it would be rude to be late.

Inside the Embassy the man in the crisp dark suit peered at me inquisitively. I smiled at him sweetly. My hair was a bird's nest, my face red. He rose from his chair, waved airily at the seat before him and relapsed into silence.

The inquisition began. What exactly was the purpose of my visit? How long precisely would I be staying? What were the names and addresses of my friends? Would I be travelling alone? If with someone, what was the name, date of birth and profession of that person? What were my political views? Did I have a criminal record? Had I considered Dubai as an alternative? It would be a lot safer and just as hot. His voice, calm and measured, became more agitated as he failed to receive the answers he wanted. Why did I really want to go, anyway? My secret was safe with him. I could tell him anything. He had my best interests at heart.

'Perhaps you should wait,' he said at last as if in climax. 'Give it a year or two. Better still, three. Best of all, forget the idea altogether.'

I fished the small, leather-bound volume from my pocket and slid it across the table. It was a family heirloom, and I had sworn on my life to take care of it. It was my cherished wish, I told him, to follow in the footsteps of its author, my great-great-great-grandfather. Thomas Thomson, a botanist, had visited Afghanistan in 1842 to study the flora of the country. The story went that he had been captured by local tribesmen in Ghazni, where he had narrowly escaped being sold into slavery. In the book was mentioned an orchid known as the *sahlab*, used in medicinal preparations and reported to be an aphrodisiac. It had also been sold on the streets of London, where it was known as *salep*. A shop in Fleet Street had sold a drink made from the bulb of the plant that it described as a 'delicacy beyond the luxury of China'.

He casually flicked the pages, peered at one narrowly, then slid the book back over. 'No good,' he said firmly.

There was nothing for it but to play my trump card, as in truth it was my only one. I handed over the letter from Mr Noor, bearing a name and an address in Kabul where I would be welcome at any time.

Sensing defeat, he shrugged his shoulders. 'Whatever you do, don't go walking alone in the city,' I thought I heard him say, but I was already out of the door.

CHAPTER 2

'Where Your Heart Goes, There Your Feet will Go'

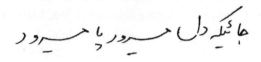

The plane was stuffy, packed and late. Women in full veils sat by others wearing mini skirts. Men in smart business suits ordered alcohol beside turbaned ones clicking prayer beads. Everyone was squashed.

The chatter died down, the obligatory screaming baby finally lulled to sleep by the hum of the engines. I traced my finger around the wing through the glass. Guilt ate at me like a canker. Memories of the bomb blast, of my cowardice, began haunting me. Others best forgotten from my past were tormenting me.

By two a.m. we had landed in Dubai. In the transit lounge, people squeezed into moulded plastic seats designed to stop them from lying down, near shop windows boasting dog shampoos, jars of saffron sugar needles and posters of models in bikinis, Hollywood's burka. Every seat was taken. Asian ladies bent in *tête à tête* sat beside Polish builders with bushy moustaches, between Bangladeshi pilgrims and Africans in Adidas T-shirts.

I sat down on the carpet pondering its greyness. Could this possibly be the Dubai I had heard about, the epitome

of extravagance, fast cars, fast women and slow construc-
tion sites, where it was illegal to kiss in public, be gay, or
share a flat with your boyfriend, where sex outside
marriage could cost you a year in jail? I was travelling from
a world of excess to one of scarcity, but as we drove to the
plane in the shabby old minibus, it didn't feel like it.

By six a.m. the chatter had subsided. Only the lone
voice of the baby, who had woken and begun crying again,
cut through the silence like acid.

Outside the window the sun lit the clouds. For a while
I watched the shadow of the plane as it filed through the
desert beneath us. The land soon became crenellated,
violently twisted as if by some great unseen hand.
Tributary streams gleamed like nerve-endings. Then the
rock smoothed out. A city shone out of the dust, domes
bobbing in a sea of yellow ochre structures, hard edges, and
craters. Blocks of buildings and settlements seemed to rise
organically out of the land itself: a burnt-out tank, a
battered hangar, wrecks of airplanes, a broken lorry, a
graveyard of scrap.

The plane corkscrewed down to the runway. Giant
hoardings loomed into view bearing the faces of President
Karzai and Massoud, the Afghan war hero. Women, pale-
faced and silent, fumbled for their scarves and covered their
heads. Hastily I did the same, unsure how to wrap mine so
it did not fall. There, now I had it. How weird it felt.

Walking across the almost melting tarmac, the heat
crisped my face, the sky a luminous Yves Klein blue, the
light so incandescent it made my eyes water. In the
terminal building lay a rabbit warren of passageways where
pipes and cables poked menacingly from the walls. The

arrivals hall was a mass of neon, peeling walls and concrete breeze-blocks. Turbans clustered around the baggage carousel like vultures. Cloaked women greeted packages like old friends. There were bundles tied with string and cellophane, makeshift suitcases bound with cardboard and sticky tape, strange bubble-wrapped objects, a push-chair no one had bothered to wrap at all. Two men fought over a black bag until the hole spat out an identical one, and they bowed, all courtesies. Everyone clambered, pushed and squeezed until, finally, the carousel spluttered and died.

There was no respite from the stares of customs officers and a marathon of forms, signings and stampings. The customs officer scrutinised my passport, stared with raised eyebrows at my face and then at the sheet of paper in front of him. What was I doing here? Was I not an aid-worker? Was I not a news reporter? Was I not working for my government? There must be some explanation. He stared at me harder. I was surely a spy, and a rather cunning one at that, he said. As he finally waved me through, I couldn't help taking it as a compliment. Then again, it might have had something to do with the bottle of perfume I had just handed him for his wife. Lucky he didn't speak French. It was called *Agent Provocateur*.

There was a dreamlike quality to those first steps. How should I walk? Should I stroll or scurry? Should I smile or look down? More to the point, how could I carry my enormous suitcase unaided? I needn't have worried; I was spoiled for choice among the small boys eager to help in return for *bakshishi,* a token tip or payment. I had never seen children's faces like these, young and old at the same time, eyelashes mascara'd with filthy thick dust. Swept up in the chaotic throng that rushed to the exit, I hadn't time to make a choice. At the dusty mouth, giant billboards advertised instant soup and mobile phones. I sat down on my case and waited as the strange new world moved around me. Then suddenly a figure was bending, studying me with sympathy. 'Taxi?' I lifted my head, squinting through my fingers. 'Yes,' I said thankfully, and followed him through the crowd.

The veteran 1963 Ford Cortina was painted orange to blend with the rusty patches. Inside it looked like a festive grotto. Bells tinkled, tassels dangled, stickers of cartoon characters and political figures jostled. An amulet dangled from the rearview mirror, and a blue eye to ward off evil. The driver grabbed my suitcase and lobbed it into the back. He darted before me, opening the door like an English gentleman.

Away from the airport's razor-wire hedgerows, the traffic grew thick. A river of cars blasted frantically their horns, while bicycles wove their way through the jam like silverfish. Ahead lay curls of barbed wire, sandbags and blast barriers, wire-mesh cubes lined with dirt-filled poly bags. All were guarded by heavily armed soldiers and policemen in blue uniforms.

My first impressions were of a ruined and devastated place, of grave mounds and mud, of buckled structures and scorched patches – a diseased, indebted, collapsed world: the scenery of war.

Kabul itself felt like a city full of paradoxes. Craters yawned between cracked mud buildings. A muddle of dirt, rubble and war scrap jostled with gleaming glass blocks and transmission towers. Between boarded-up buildings lay walls pitted with bullet holes. Cables hung like giant spider webs. Open drains ran down the streets littered with decaying rubbish. Elsewhere it looked like a showcase of kitsch, of glittering fantasy mansions, poppy palaces born of opium profits and war booty. There were flashes of beauty. Amid war scrap and suicide bombs, vines adorned espaliers. Plastic flowers lay on the counter of a street kiosk. Scrawled verses of the Qur'an decorated walls over doorways. Police crowded the streets, their guns decorated with floral patterns and pink hearts, the dashboards of their cars covered with silk flowers.

The dust was ubiquitous. It lay thick on the cars, the buildings and the walls, in the folds of women's veils and the wrinkles of men's faces. Eyebrows were caked in it. Eyelashes were mascara'd with it.

The driver was called Omar, named after his hero, the film star Omar Sharif. I strained to make sense of his salvo of questions. There were mystifying twangs punctuated with Arabic-sounding gutturals. I guessed the jist by his eager gesticulating and responded by admiring his extra-large turban. He glowed with pride and the rest of the journey went effortlessly.

Omar delivered a diatribe, arms swirling erratically as he wove his way through the mass of old bangers. 'How can anyone think straight about anything when all they can think about is the fighting?' he huffed. If wasn't one thing it was another: the weather, the politics, the women . . . It was a mess. The government was useless; its areas of control had shrunk to tiny fortified islands in the cities. Most of the problems boiled down to bribery. Clerks demanded money to stamp forms, police asked drivers to pay to enter cities, authorities sold government land to their cronies for luxury-housing projects, security officials colluded with the drug-traffickers they were supposed to be catching. No one cared about the poor. There was no work for many Afghans, and the people were angry that the Western reconstruction projects failed to provide jobs for them. What few jobs there had been were taken by foreigners, which was the best recruiting strategy for the Taliban, and the perfect opportunity for insurgents. He let out a sigh, and his engine juddered as if in sympathy. At least, he said, he had one thing to be grateful for.

'What is that?' I asked.

'My sunny disposition, of course,' he said, with a stunning display of yellowing teeth.

We had arrived. The taxi drew up near a sad-looking doorway. The hotel building looked quite lost in the rubble. 'It's *special*,' said Omar, and from the look on his face I had no reason to doubt it. As I hopped out of the back, he brandished a card with languorous writing. Tilted slightly, it read 'Have a nice day' in English. Normally he specialised in driving elderly and disabled people, but in my case he would make an exception.

We said our goodbyes and as I crossed over the street a truck stormed past and nearly ran over me.

Behind the front desk the innkeeper was sleeping. He carefully adjusted his expertly folded turban and opened his eyes. He looked around sheepishly. 'You are alone?' he said shiftily.

'Yes, please,' I said, 'I would like a single room.'

'Fifty dollars' he said in English, still looking around for my absent husband.

I picked up my bags and began turning away.

'But for you,' he added indifferently, 'thirty.'

'I will be staying for a while,' I said, dropping the bags again.

'Twenty dollars,' he said thinly.

I was too tired to argue. I handed over my passport and he took it and squinted at it. Then he slipped it away in the drawer behind him. As I watched it disappear, I wondered if I would ever see it again.

Upstairs the corridor was grimy. I wobbled the key in the ill-fitting door, which opened into a sad sort of room. A lonely candle wilted on the bedside table like a tulip, and some flies had made themselves a burial ground in the ceiling fan, which was dead owing to the absence of electricity. The few bits of furniture were nailed to the floor and on the short mattress lay a pile of dirty blankets and the vestiges of a mosquito net that was, on closer inspection, an old net curtain. The sheets were nylon, and a pubic hair lay on the pillow, which had the texture of a sandbag. Suddenly the plush hotel in the high-security compound option seemed rather appealing.

There was more. A dark, pungent smell was emanating from the tiny adjacent chamber. I tiptoed over the slippery floor towards a menacing-looking hole and as I flicked on the light switch a fluorescent strip buzzed like the demented fly that circled it. Further investigation into what had in the most generous terms been described as the bathroom revealed the rest of its glories. There was a sink, stained and broken. Something was growing in the corner, towards which a few spiders with blotchy bodies were rushing as if they were being summoned. A brownish liquid trickled from the plastic tube grafted on to an old water pipe which I guessed was the shower, and a large puddle on the floor suggested the water tank was leaking. At least, I hoped it was water.

My armpits were sweaty. I edged past the bare wiring dangling around the broken mirror, climbed tentatively under the so-called shower and turned the knob, which immediately went into spasm. Defeated, I gave up and sprayed myself with deodorant. I spread my sleeping bag on the nylon sheets, picked off the hair, and collapsed on the bed.

It was a very long time before I finally dropped off. Several hours later I woke with a jolt, with the room shaking violently. I peered through the window, as a convoy of lorries thundered past in the street. The din abated, and my eyelids grew heavy. Soothed by the drip of the lullaby cistern, I slept like a baby.

CHAPTER 3

'Walls Have Mice and Mice have Ears'

دیوار ها موش دارند و موش ها گوش

A curious sound was floating in my head. As I drifted back into consciousness the single, twisting note was joined by other disturbing moans. There was something else, too, a frantic sort of scuttling. I put the pillow back over my head and tried to ignore it, but it was useless. Through the large holes in the curtains a shaft of white light was beaming straight onto me. As I stepped out of bed, the muezzin stopped calling and the mouse hurried off.

I approached the bathroom with some trepidation. Tiptoeing around the cables and avoiding the hole, I turned on the shower, which hissed like a snake. A jet of brown water spurted straight across the floor and missed me entirely. I hopped away fast, almost skidding in the damp patches. As I dressed and knotted my headscarf I glanced in the mirror. I felt glad to be unrecognisable. I hardly knew myself.

I opened the door and walked quietly down the stairway. The desk was deserted. Outside the hotel I sighed with relief and immediately began coughing. The air stank openly of diesel and faeces.

I was meeting my contact at ten. That left two whole hours to get my bearings. I fished out the phone card and punched in the number. The display stared back in silence. What if I missed this Tariq person? I was sweating just thinking about it.

As walked down the street I picked out signs for 'World Top Gym' and an advert for 'Attraction, the New Luxury Fragrance for Women'. A message over a doorway read 'Be happy all the time.'

I was already drawing attention to myself. Eyes glanced shiftily. Heads peeped stealthily. A photographer peeked from a family of field cameras. Soldiers in khaki watched policemen in blue, but all united in their stares at the foreign woman.

I took out my map and tried to ignore them. I was not far down when a taxi drew up. Regrettably it wasn't Omar's. The driver began studying me. 'Thank you,' I said shyly, 'I'm happy just walking.' In dismay he drove off. Further along the way the taxi slowed down again. I climbed in the back and when we drew to a halt, we had digressed to the outskirts of the city, but I had learnt something from that journey. Kabul had no scenic routes.

As finally we returned I handed over the fare. The driver began his excuses, sighing wearily at the money. Was that *all* I was giving him? He was expecting at least double that. The price was a fair one. The checkpoints took so long it was halving his earnings. His family was starving. He had seventeen mouths to feed. Petrol was expensive. Petrol had gone up. Petrol was hardly available these days. Petrol was controlled by the Taliban. He puffed up his chest and took a deep breath. 'It's *foreigner* inflation!' he hollered, before finally slumping over the steering wheel.

I reached into my pocket and paid him what he asked for. I hadn't enough change, so I paid him some extra – in British pound coins.

★ ☽ ★

The old quarter was a labyrinth of narrow streets and mud-walled passageways. Men wearing turbans carried songbirds in cages. Traders were shouting. Horns were blaring. Motorcycle brakes were screeching. Tea was being brewed on street corners in kettles. Boys bashed at metal, making buckets and saucepans. Techno and rap blared from over-loud radios. Street children were working, scattering the path with smiles in the absence of flowers. Some carried water canisters to refill bottles, or cloths to polish shoes. Others burnt *spand,* an aromatic herb, for good luck – all in return for just a few *afghanis.*

The garden at the teahouse was a tinderbox of dust, the dull square yard made gloomier by its walls. A boy, lithe-limbed and with blue-green eyes, was sitting on the ground. He looked far too young to be the one I was meeting. I was just about to leave when the boy raised his head. As he beamed a great grin, I felt the gloom suddenly evaporating. It was him, after all.

Our series of greetings met with a range of averted glances. I went to shake his hand, then checked myself. Touching would be too much.

'*Salaam aleikum*, peace be with you.'

'*Aleikum salaam*, and with you.'

'*Al Hamdu' l'Illa*, thanks be to God. *Haale Shoma chetor*

25

ast, how is your health?'

'*Khoob astom, tashakur*, I am well, thank you.'

'*Madaretan, padaretaan, khaanawaadetaan?* Is your mother well, your father, your family well?'

'*Al Hamdu l'Illah, khoob hastand*, Praise God, they are well.'

We sat on a rug the colour of ox blood and drank tea from small glasses. Tea was good for the health, said Tariq, the sweeter the better, the more honoured the guest. Water was bad for the circulation and should be avoided at all costs.

The questions landed with force and velocity: 'Who is the president in your country? Is he as useless as Karzai? What do you think of Afghanistan? Is it more beautiful than your country? Where is your brother, your uncle, your father? Have they let you come alone here? Why did you come here, anyway?'

'It's complicated,' I said. He didn't press me to tell him more and I was grateful for it.

I handed him the note from Mr Noor and he opened it, rubbing his chin as if to stroke a beard that had not had time to grow.

'Perhaps you are a spy?' he said mischievously.

I gazed at him vacantly.

'Pity,' he sighed, dwelling on how much more exciting it would have been. He could tell just from looking at me that I wasn't one. As he hung his head lamely, I guessed what he really meant was they wouldn't send a woman.

Tariq spoke quickly and loudly. At times he seemed overtaken by panic, then he relaxed and fell silent. There was something about him I couldn't quite fathom. As he looked at me uncertainly, I suspected the feeling was mutual. He seemed, by Afghan standards, to be well educated, and wiser than his years, but as birthdays were not celebrated in Afghanistan, even he did not know exactly how old he was. He must have been at least twenty, he thought, as he had spent three years studying English at Kabul University. He wanted to be a great man. In the mean time, he did a motley assortment of jobs: taxi driver, administrator at the hospital, government adviser. He was a good Muslim, he said, whatever that meant; and, like all Afghans, he was a poet. He wanted to marry, but he couldn't afford the bride price. Women were so expensive these days.

He spoke of the city as a badly wounded animal; of the divide between the haves and the have-nots as an ever-deepening chasm. It was the fault of the foreigners who vowed to rebuild the city and broke their promises. There was electricity only in a few districts, and even then it was only every other night and just for a few hours. Most homes had no running water, and Kabul still lacked a sewage system. It was an arduous existence, where dreams became nightmares, where everyone watched what they said and who they talked to, where murder was an everyday occurrence. Nobody felt safe. The police themselves were responsible for robberies linked to big criminal gangs. The government supported the criminals, and you never knew whom you were talking to.

The Taliban were growing stronger. Their parallel system of governing the land was sweeping a country where the official lawmakers were seen as corrupt and ineffective. They were a whirlwind militia, a confederation of young men who would fight to the death. They came from all tribal backgrounds. They were criminals and religious hardliners, linked by their anger at the West and, in particular, at American foreign policy. The mood of despair had played into the hands of those who saw themselves as an alternative source of justice.

Their leaders were spiritual, not motivated by personal gain or glory, but by the determination that the enemies of Allah should lay down their arms. They believed in military piety, in the name of Allah to restore peace and freedom from tyranny. They had learnt from their experience of war with the Soviets and their brothers in Iraq. Although in the early years of the occupation the insurgency had been fragmented and chaotic, now the campaign was structured, a sophisticated network of military and civilian leadership. The Taliban would win the war because they moved silently. They used surprise. They altered their form like clever chameleons, moving secretly among the people. They were invisible, as Lawrence of Arabia had said of the Arabs – like vapour.

'You haven't been out, have you?' he whispered then, glancing over his shoulder to make sure no one was listening in on us.

'It wasn't very far.'

He was shaking his head at me. I should never walk in the city alone, I could trust no one. I should never take photos, single myself out as a tourist. Ideally, I should never walk in the city at all. It was a den of spies, suicide-bombers and hostage-takers. The Taliban mingled, unseen, a hidden threat. Secret police lurked in every group; children were trained to spy and report on foreigners.

Kidnapping had become a daily occurrence and had become a clever business. Some gangs even used police uniforms and police vehicles in their abductions. They covered their tracks. A victim would be taken and tortured for weeks until a ransom was demanded. If the sum went unpaid, death was the outcome. A foreigner could be worth up to $200,000, even $500,000. All foreigners were rich, and they could afford it. Already a number of hostages had been executed.

Seeing the fear writ large across my face he stopped and tried to comfort me. He was sure Allah was with me, but as an extra precaution he himself would be happy to be my guide and translator. He could tell how badly I needed someone.

There remained the small matter of his remuneration. If I offered too much he would be offended, too little and he would be insulted. I scribbled a figure on his notepad and he collapsed with laughter. I doubled it and he looked embarrassed. I wondered if I had offended him. How could I thank him? Before I had finished the question I wished I hadn't asked. He wanted to meet the Pope of England, he said, but if that was not possible, then he would settle for the President. Above all, he said, gazing wistfully into the distance, his dearest wish was to make the pilgrimage to Mecca.

'Pay me what you think I am worth,' he grinned finally, as we decided to leave it open. Only now did I understand that phrase Kipling once uttered: 'You can't buy an Afghan, only rent one.'

CHAPTER 4

'No Rose is Without Thorns'

هیچ گلی بی خار نیست

By five to six I had washed my face and unpacked my things. There were blobs down my legs where mosquitoes had feasted. My feet were blistered and my nose was a strawberry, succombing to an infection due to the bad air. I felt ashamed to complain about them. These specks of discomfort were miniscule compared to the great suffering around me. The wounds of war were immeasurable, the hardships of poverty unimaginable.

As I opened the door, my tunic began tweeting. I dug in my pocket to pull out the phone, but it was silent and blank. I slumped on the mattress and read for a while, kept company by my room mates – the beetles and the mice, and a solitary, brave cockroach who had made his way out of the bathroom and was on his own epic adventure. I comforted myself with the thought there were no rats. For the time being, anyway.

It was about half an hour before there came a tap on the window. Taking care not to dislodge the rag that plugged a hole in the pane, I glanced down at the street and Tariq's face beamed back. I ran down to meet him.

'You're not staying *there*, are you?' he said immediately. Word had it the place was run by the secret police. It was run by Tajiks and you could never trust a Tajik. He would try and sort out a Pashtun one for me. Pashtuns were the best. When it came to foreigners, they were tolerant.

The street was chaotic, but he seemed oblivious to the mayhem, babbling in Dari I could barely keep up with. He resorted to English, proudly pointing at his vehicle like a father with a baby. I paused to do a double-take. It was a relic from the Russian military invasion, he said. He had acquired it from an army friend. Afghanistan was a big country, he had a big heart, and he needed a big car, but unfortunately he couldn't afford one.

'Is it safe?' I asked warily, eyeing the connection between bike and car which looked as if it might snap at any moment. Tariq ignored me. With not a whisker of an alternative, I climbed in and prayed. A swirl of dust, a roar of thunder, and we were off, dodging the holes, honking the horn, and shouting to make ourselves audible.

The road was fraught with the roar of trucks and the braying of donkeys. We wove through the jam, past traffic policemen gesticulating wildly, and children with matted hair and snotty noses, some carrying firewood on their shoulders, others leaning in poses copied from soldiers whose rifles seemed as familiar as their milk bottles. One walked in the the road. Arm lifted in the air in a robotic gesture, he wove between the cars with a concertina of phone-cards. 'Shouldn't we stop and help?' went strangely unanswered. Tariq just shrugged his shoulders, as if there was nothing unusual in it.

A sea of mud rooftops lapped the hillside. Houses were

connected by a labyrinth of pathways. The light drifted, in places gleaming on the mud like liquid. Men swept pavements with witches' brooms. Children skipped like mountain goats. Burkas struggled with heavy bundles drooping over their shoulders. There were no trees, just dirt and rubble and carcasses of houses, featureless and desolate. Buildings lay rotting, bombed and abandoned. Pipes grovelled in the dust, mangled and twisted, as if they were trying to hide themselves.

Tariq's house was no different from the rest. Its high mud walls were embedded with shrapnel. Children peeked round the doorway, wily and alert. I smiled and they laughed. Inside it was gloomy. Greasy shoulders had left their mark on the walls, bare except for a photo sporting bushy moustaches and shrubbery beards. Carpets covered a floor of bare earth. A selection of rifles was propped up in the corner and a lonely plastic swan on a paper doily adorned the window ledge. Beyond lay a small yard where a Judas tree dripped a with green that glowed against the brown of its surroundings. At the back of the house shadowy figures flitted, like ghosts. I guessed they must have been the women.

The room had cushions round the sides. Water hissed from a blackened kettle over wood that burned brightly. Wafts of smoke hung in the air like nebulae. Faces carved with character expressed pride, strength, and courage. Men of maturity sat cross-legged or squatted, puffing their pipes and chewing tobacco. They wore turbans and tunics of beige, creams and greens, a palette of muted hues to tone in with their mood. One, snowy bearded, stood up and bowed deeply. It was Tariq's Uncle Ahmed, head of the household. By his stately demeanour I could tell he was not to be argued with. The floodgates of language broke forth. The accent was so impenetrable that at first I caught nothing. Fortunately a smile was a smile in any language.

'You are a Muslim?' he asked graciously.

The circle went quiet.

'No,' I said sheepishly. Better to say I was a Yezidi devil-worshipper than admit to being a Christian.

'And where is your husband?'

A hush filled the room as I lowered my head. Better to stay quiet than admit I didn't have one.

'*Hich goolee bi khaar neest*,' he said sadly. It meant 'no rose is without thorns'.

The men drank tea, eyeing me cautiously. It felt strange and unnerving. All the while they talked animatedly. As they spoke I snatched glimpses – of Islamic history as if it had happened last week; of the Prophet Muhammad as if he were a member of their family. They mourned long and deep, about which of their relatives had died, who they had known who'd lost limbs. They reflected bitterly, about the occupation, of the suffering and horrors that had bonded them in unspoken ways. They were poor but they were honest. They were not ashamed of their poor shoes. At least they had some. They were lucky to be alive. Hundreds of people were being killed every day, women and children among them. The husbands and fathers who survived were unemployed, and if they had work they were paid starvation wages while foreigners were stealing their land and insulting them. They'd been betrayed – by Karzai and by life.

Later that evening I slipped on my shoes, turned in a

small gesture of courtesy away from the door, and Mr Omar came to collect me in the taxi. In the darkness, figures lurked, squatting and standing at the roadside. Others in doorways smoked opium. Soldiers clustered round a fire or a building, crouching, hugging their rifles, orange dots of their cigarettes snuffed out one by one as they became hidden by a corner or a wall. A flock of doves was turning through the darkening skies, shooed off its course by the buzz of a helicopter and a distant crackle. Someone appeared to have set off a firework. We passed barefoot children standing on boxes, not sure what to make of the spectacle, but it was the adult faces that bore the most trepidation. They were familiar with a different type of firework – Tomahawks, stealth bombs and artillery shells, the rockets of war.

In the sanctuary of my hotel room, I ripped off my scarf and saw the message from my mother on the display of my phone. There was no reception, and I couldn't retrieve it. I lit a candle and in the glow reached out my fingers to the pillow, feeling its emptiness. I snuffed out the flame, and was engulfed by the darkness.

★ ☽ ★

The kitchen was a secret place. It was the women's domain, where they learnt how to fashion their approach to life, how to be a woman. Afghan women were mysterious beings who lived under veils, behind curtains and walls. It was unsurprising that it had taken several days before I was allowed to go in there. Ahmed had considered the idea carefully. He himself was a liberal-minded man, interested in Western culture. It was only later that I learnt Tariq had bribed him. He'd promised I would give him English lessons.

The light was scarce in the small, dark room. Just a tiny window by the sink scattered fairy sunbeams into the heart of it, but even that looked out at a tatty mud wall. The window was a hole with a piece of plastic sheeting. Glass was for rich people. Mint, basil, coriander, and cooking smells mingled with the stench of open drains, and half-dressed little ones crawled around the floor. There were a few bits and bobs around – a wood-burning stove, a sink, a water tank for when the supply was running, and a table bearing vestiges of flour from the ritual of bread-making. Dust swirled in eddies in the inadequate fireplace. On the wall hung a burka.

An older woman, stern-featured, offered me tea laced with cardamom, while a young one watched, pale, with beautiful dark eyes. Their clothes were loose-fitting – dresses and trousers in pink, red and green. The older lady was Tariq's mother. Her name was Sohaila. The young one, Maryam, was Tariq's younger sister.

A stream of words poured forth, any deficiencies in language made up for by gestures. As the women spoke freely, I tried to keep up with them, catching the jist though the wonders of sign language. There were many more questions to those Tariq had posed. How could a plane travel so fast? How could we eat potatoes every day and not rice? Did I know Robert Redford? Who was the Pope of my country? Had my government sent me? Could I trust my government? Was my government as useless as their one? How much was a dowry where I came from? How is it women went to work where I came from? Could an ugly woman marry in my country? How many people could read? How many Muslims were there? Why were the soldiers here? How soon would they be leaving? Where was England anyway? I sighed with relief when the inquisition ended, at a loss to answer in English, let alone in Dari.

Sohaila was a stickler when it came to the routine of life. Her days were structured around housework, cooking and childcare, and the rituals of Islam. Every morning she rose at six o'clock sharp. She prepared bread and tea for the family. After that she would wake her eight-year-old son and youngest three daughters, gently placing the palm of her hand on their foreheads and reciting the opening verse of the Qur'an, uttering their names more and more loudly until, with little Basma, she would be forced to bang on the tin drum she had received as a birthday gift from Tariq. As soon as they were awake, she would recite a verse from the Qur'an to protect them all from the evil eye.

She worried constantly, dancing round her memories with youthful agility. Where had her looks gone? Had she been a good enough mother? Could she have done more? There were so many deaths, a neighbour, and her own husband who popped out for a loaf of bread and never came back. When he died it felt as if she lost her life too. There was so much guilt, so many feelings of unworthiness. You survived and they didn't. She now sought solace in small things, a flower, a smile. She did not forget, just became better at distracting herself. She tried to stay strong for the sake of the family. How could you heal a broken heart? How could you put back together a broken life?

The one thing that gave her hope was the children. The reason to have little ones was the future.

At the mention of babies Maryam rolled her eyes. At just sixteen, she was already engaged. It was to be a marriage of convenience. They were poor, he was lonely. As head of the family, her uncle had wished only, as all parents did, for her to find a suitable husband. Ahmed had been clear on the subject. Women belonged at home. Girls without husbands would be pitied or shunned. She was the family's greatest prize, but she had independent ideas of which he didn't approve and which he tolerated out of respect for his brother. It was just a phase she would grow out of. 'Maryam, when are you ever going to learn to be a proper Afghan woman?' he would ask. By that he meant tying herself to the kitchen sink.

Since her father had died, her uncle had acted as his stand-in, undertaking all the negotiations, but it was her mother who was the real matchmaker. When it came to marriage, she had all the power. She had her ways of checking out the applicants, and dismissed those she saw as inappropriate, informing her brother-in-law only about the short list.

With Maryam's looks, they had their pick of the bunch, and there had been no shortage of suitors. The selection process had taken ages. In the end, one had emerged the clear favourite. Word had it that Zaki Hassan was an honest man, a good man. His family came from Kunduz, the city in the north that had been a hub of unrest. He was a good catch for Maryam. He was an Uzbek. It could have been worse, said Sohaila, who would have preferred it if he had been Pashtun, as they were. He could have been wild and lawless like the Hazaras. Hazaras were Shi'a. They were seriously deluded people.

To begin with, Maryam had come round to the idea with a degree of defiance. She had made a list of objections. She would not be ashamed to have a baby daughter. She would not obey her husband's every demand. She would not walk four steps behind him. She would not give herself to him if he forced her. Above all, she would not give up her new job which gave her life meaning. It was not long before she realised that such reservations were futile. At that point she submitted. In her heart she held on to her dream. Islam held that as soon as a baby was born an angel wrote its destiny on its forehead, and on hers had been '*moallem*'. It meant teacher.

CHAPTER 5

'Ask the Truth from a Child'

حقیقت را از طفل بپرس

The shabby sign bore noble words: '*Elm wa honar shoma ra pesh mebarad*', Knowledge and Skills Take You Further'. A few birds were twittering in the plane trees as if they had heard something and wanted to pass it on. Perhaps word had got around that a foreign woman was walking alone there. Maybe the police had tipped them off already.

The guard looked quite stern, but it was the little birds whose flapping and chirruping he seemed mostly to mistrust. He watched them especially as he reluctantly waved me through the gate.

Inside the school the long, thin corridor was decorated with Disney cartoons, and hygiene and safety drills in big red letters. The headmaster's office was a box room with a few chairs standing around. Mr Hussein, a tall man with a stoop acquired from a habit of bending down to everyone, looked at me searchingly. The wars, combined with the habit of questioning and being questioned, had given him a suspicious manner.

His own trauma of losing two of his brothers in a roadside bomb attack helped him understand the problems of his pupils, he said. They were the lucky ones. Many children did not go to school at all and many more were orphaned. Textbooks were so badly printed and so scarce they had to be shared among three pupils, sometimes more. In the summer they boiled. In the winter, they froze. There weren't enough classrooms or teachers to hold separate classes for the youngest ones. A makeshift wall separated boys and girls, but it was too low and the boys peeked over the top at the girls. Girls were not allowed to run, laugh out loud, or look at the boys, but the boys waited for them to pass and stuck notes in their hands or pulled faces at them. They knew it was naughty, but it didn't stop them.

Most of the children had witnessed terrible atrocities. They had paralysing depressions, mood-swings and sudden out-of-control tantrums. Eyes welled with tears, attention spans were limited. There were ethnic problems, too, between Pashto and Dari speakers. Outside school, they helped their mothers, begging or selling things. When they grew up, they wanted to be fighters, and although many didn't know the difference between eat and play, they knew the names and sounds of all the guns, rockets, mortars and missiles, how to put out fires, how to give first aid, how to lie down on the floor in the event of a bomb. They had learnt the greatest art, that of survival. They were the lucky ones, he said. Education was for the privileged.

The children sat cross-legged in a semi-circle, dressed in pyjama clothes, tatty and mostly too big for them. The little bodies had old faces; some were without a hand, or part of a leg. They were restless, yawning, some with dark rings beneath their eyes, some with scars from infections from sand–fly bites, one or two limping from polio.

Maryam waved me to sit down. On her left hand she had a girl finger-puppet and on her right a boy puppet. She was acting as though the puppets were really talking, telling the children that the puppets were very shy and explaining they had had bad things happen to them. The children looked concerned. They really wanted to help the puppets. As Maryam's voice grew softer, they were all ears. 'Would you like to help them by drawing a picture of something sad that has happened to you?' she asked.

Silence fell suddenly. Little faces looked lost. Crayons and paper were handed round, tiny fingers clasping, eyes gazing trustingly as if the world might be a good place after all. One child drew a mother holding a child's hand, with fountains of tears streaming from the mother's eyes. Another drew guns and soldiers, and people lying on the ground. Most drew faces filled with sadness.

'The puppets are wondering if you would like to get rid of the pictures?' asked Maryam, her voice reassuring.

'Yes! Yes!' cried the children, tearing up the pictures and stamping their feet on them. A waste-paper basket was brought round and the pictures were thrown away.

'Now they are asking you to do happy drawings,' she said, making the puppets bob up and down, bending them towards her ears. 'You can draw anything, something you like, something good that has happened, or someone you love . . . '

The children began drawing, eyes glittering like full moons. There were pictures of food, donkeys, camels and birds. '*Akse hai khosh! Akse hai khosh!* Happy pictures! Happy pictures!' they all cried.

'Would you like to keep these pictures?' she asked, after they had finished.

'*Bale! Bale!* Yes! Yes!' they cried again.

'I have one more favour to ask of you,' said Maryam. 'I'd like to give each of you a puppet and ask if you would take care of it.' She reached into the plastic bag beside her chair and gave each child its own puppet. As she did so she placed the hand holding the puppet on the child's heart. Some of them kissed the puppets; others spoke to them like friends or confidants to whom they could tell their secrets.

And that was how I left them that day, their faces full of love and joy. I didn't stay longer or I might have learnt something. The next lesson was about mines.

CHAPTER 6

'He is Riding the Donkey,
but he has Lost the Donkey'

بالای خـــــرسوار است دخـــــرراگم کرده

'Try it on,' said Maryam, picking out a blue one. The burka was alive, a scary blue monster with ripples and pleats. I wrestled with the nylon, and at last pulled it on, wobbling round like a child in a Hallowe'en costume. Inside it was stifling, the material so thick I inhaled my own breath. I couldn't see anything.

Sohaila tugged it down, until at last the cap stayed firm. The hair was, above all, the most important thing to hide. It was the root of all temptation, she said. I smiled back, but the smile never made it through the mesh.

I wanted to know the truth. Was the burka a window to the face, or a prison for one? What was it like not to have to think about how you looked? What should I wear today? What should I do with my hair? What make-up shall I put on? For the women of Afghanistan these questions were meaningless. Do I have enough to feed my family? How can I give my children warm clothing and shoes for the winter? These were the pressing concerns. Vanity was eclipsed by suffering and poverty.

We stepped out, pleats swinging, one round burka in cornflower blue with white tips, one slim one, a third stumbling at the rear.

Like a blinkered horse, I fixed a point on the horizon, since left and right were out of range. I guessed it was deliberate. A woman's gaze should be focused on her husband. Not that I imagined she could see him. I was amazed she was able to see anything.

As I squinted through my visor, shapes loomed into view. Things huddled in heaps. Objects dangled from poles. If I concentrated hard, I could just about guess them. In the women's bazaar there was everything you could want for a kitchen – pots and pans, plastic and metal, spoons, bowls, great saucepans with lids and without, rolling pins, pestles and mortars, and measuring pots. Sacks brimmed with vegetables. Boxes teamed with nighties. Baskets displayed bras with polyester cups the size of small hammocks. All were framed by the criss-cross of my visor.

With vision impaired, other senses felt heightened. The aroma of kebabs sizzling on charcoal smelt more enticing. The music of Bollywood sounded louder. Things took on a surreal quality. Bundles seemed to move through the crowd as if magically suspended on figures and animals that remained unseen.

As women were stuck with the burka, they became creative with it. They were conscious of the shapes they cut. They swung the folds provocatively as they walked. Touches of individuality made a fleeting impression: a dash of kohl and turquoise on a heavily cloaked face, sewn-on jewels and braid, shiny gold rings on elegant hands, bright red toenails and sandals peeking out below. It was all about the detail.

If a man saw a burka he knew if she was beautiful. It was the way that she moved and the poise with which she held herself. Of course, it wasn't a fashion show. A husband recognised his wife because he bought her shoes for her. And when a burka begged for money, it hid her shame.

I had been struggling to keep up. Voluminous and heavy, the burka kept catching. With the over-long hem, it was inevitable I would trip. When I dragged myself up again, the others had gone. Desperate to get my bearings, I lifted the front and looked round, but there was a bevy of burkas and all looked identical.

Defeated, I gave up. Hidden under the nylon and blind as a bat, I had lost all points of reference. And I was lost. I hoisted it off and screwed it into my bag, then tightened my headscarf and made my way home. I felt fortunate. Afghan women had no such choice.

★ ☽ ★

It was an unassuming doorway, a small plume of smoke the only suggestion of what lay within. The *hammam* was the only place where the women could relax and gossip. They didn't get out much, taking to heart the Prophet's advice to stay in their houses. They even prayed at home rather than in the mosque, going there only on special occasions.

Bathing was a fixture, an event, an occasion. The walls were guardians of the deepest secrets. 'Cleanliness was part of the faith,' said Islam, but it was the spirit that really counted. Purity of body brought purity of soul, and I could tell they thought I could do with it.

Through the net of the burka I saw a dowdy-looking

room. The walls were bare concrete and there was litter on the floor. It looked a far cry from the great *hammams* I had read about, the sumptuous luxury, the elaborate rituals begun long before Islam.

It was all about pampering. Bathers would undress in comfort, by broad, deep seats covered with rush mats or silk rugs. From the cloakroom, they would pass into bathing rooms filled with cold water, before moving on to a central room where the water was tepid. Later they would be sprayed with piping-hot water and a dry room for sweating, before an attendant would come and rub them with a glove of fine cloth.

Heads would be smeared with mud, then rinsed and dried. Feet would be scrubbed with special stones and hair would be hennaed. Eyebrows were defined with a paste made of sweet-smelling incense, nut oil and yellow arsenic or copper sulphate. Kohl was applied to the eyelids made the eyes look more beautiful. Beauty spots were sometimes added and even, according to the fashion, two symmetrical lines of fake tears to the cheeks.

The air was filled with exotic scents. Extracts of rose petals, orange blossom, and the flowers of jasmine, geranium, laurel or eglantine, provided the fragrances for soaps, lotions, and even the water. Amber, saffron, extracts of camomile or violets, musk, camphor, civet and sandalwood or myrtle completed the process carried out by masseurs, hairdressers and herbalists.

But that was all then. Today we were lucky to have running water.

It was time to get undressed. The women shed their burkas effortlessly, while my own became caught up and tangled. When finally I emerged it was a *frisson* of triumph. Shyly we stripped down to our undies, and as the women stared at my gleaming flesh I felt naked.

At the end of the corridor a misty scene emerged, of steaming bodies, pleats of flesh, saggy bottoms, pendulous breasts, and thighs that were flabby or muscular. Rubens-esque ladies in the tepid fog had towels knotted on their heads like turbans, gossiping furiously. The mix of hot and cold had an intoxicating effect. Imaginations drifted, daydreams were indulged, problems exchanged. Thoughts matured in reflection like fine cheeses.

A *hammam* lady was waiting, brandishing a tub of hot, thick wax. Ladies lay back as she painted it on to them. Then she stripped it all off with the force of a Sumo wrestler. Pubic hair and any body topiary, snipped, shaped or *au naturel*, was not done. Smooth all over was essential. Sohaila exposed her fuzzy legs and a forest of black hairs emerged. It was about time she had hers done, although she preferred tweezers.

We attacked our arms with plastic loofahs. Sohaila began her advice session, the steam rising to conceal our blushes, as we listened to her whisperings with the sense of pride that a young man might feel on being offered a first cigar by his father.

Now that her daughter was engaged, any ideas that girls should be ignorant about men evaporated instantly. God's law required all intimacy to be within marriage. Within marriage, everything and anything went. The Prophet himself was not at all prudish about sex. In the Prophet's words, when a husband and wife shared intimacy, it was a blessing and was rewarded, just as it would be punished if they indulged in illicit sex. One *Sunnah* held that he had said that a man should not satisfy his need of his wife until he had satisfied her need of him, though many of the men had not read that one. Nevertheless, they all took their duties seriously. They always prayed beforehand.

I had to admit to some scepticism. It was well known that some verses in the Qur'an were open to contention – that men had dominance over a woman's body; that a wife must almost worship her husband; that if wives or husbands refused each other's advances, the Prophet said the angels would curse them until morning; that a woman must never refuse her husband even on the topmost edge of a burning oven. And what about the law that had been passed recently allowing a man to starve his wife if she refused to have sex with him? That one struck us as criminal. It went against the basic human rights of women.

'Men interpret the Qur'an differently,' she said finally. It was almost solely the strict ones who believed in that way and, almost without exception, the old ones.

'Why aren't you married yet, anyway?' she asked, frowning suspiciously suddenly. They were women of principle, and it was well known that the West had no morals when it came to the sexes.

I found myself changing the subject.

'If there is no husband, who is there then to defend your honour?' said Sohaila, who was looking suitably bemused.

'Well,' I said, 'where I come from, it's normally up to a woman to defend her own honour.'

She looked at me sternly. 'A woman without a man is

as butter to the sun,' she sighed, 'and a woman without children is lost.'

We dressed, and reached for our burkas, my friends picking out theirs instantly, I making a guess as to which one was mine, grabbing it and hoping for the best.

We chatted some more, then glided down the street like walking tents, united and formless.

CHAPTER 7

'If You Sit Beside a Cooking Pot, You will Get Black'

با ماننشتی ماتووکیا و با دیگک نشتنی سـیـاه

I was growing accustomed to the flies, the heat and the dirt. At prayer times, the mosques buzzed and hummed more than ever, but where once the muezzin's call had seemed so alien to me, it now felt sweeter, gentler. I warmed to the foibles of an eccentric lifestyle, to waiting an hour for the bucket of water to boil on the stove, or reading by candlelight.

I barely batted an eyelid at the creatures that scuttled about my room and had even grown used to my stroppy shower and the blackened soap, with dried suds caking its rim as if recently frothed. I brushed my teeth with toothpaste that had Chinese writing on the tube, and after washing my clothes, I draped them over a chair as they dried and stiffened into cardboard, victims of the local washing powder.

I was coming to love spontaneous meetings caused by the lack of mobile-phone reception, and the constant interruptions that prayer presented for people going about their daily tasks. I would read poetry that seemed to have more meaning in such a troubled place. The elaborate Afghan code of manners seemed less intimidating as I was becoming more used to it. I was learning how to make speeches of good will, to become sensitive to ranking, to take care where I sat in a room, and how I entered and left it. I found myself never speaking of the future without adding the '*Inshallah*', God willing, and averting the evil eye to ward off bad luck whenever I admired or praised something.

After one or two stomach upsets I balanced what I ate with the art of a tightrope walker. I avoided the meat and lived mostly on bread. The *naan* was delicious, squidgy, sweet and melt-in-the-mouth fresh. I scribbled my thoughts at the rickety table in my hotel room; I made lists of the things the war had not destroyed: the kites, the dreams, the tea, fake Coke, cigarettes, bad driving, drugs, corruption, not forgetting the insects.

Everywhere the effects of war were startling, from people who had lost limbs, to the refugees who told stories of massacre and destruction, to the bangs and thuds of rocket fire that often shook the city. In a city with no running water, only occasional electricity, not enough food, and the constant threat of violence, I was humbled by people with far greater problems than I could have thought possible, yet who shrugged their shoulders and got on with life.

Everyone appeared to have lost someone close to them. Everyone struggled, but somehow they survived. What use complaining about the air when there was nothing else to breathe, they would say. The lack of sanitation was taken for granted; open sewers running down streets were normal. There was not enough medical aid to go around, and no one could remember a time when there wasn't a war on.

All this had a profound effect on me, as I suspected it did on everyone who visited the country. I liked the Afghans hugely. I admired them and respected them. I found them proud, brave, as kind as they were canny, with deep humanity, and an instinct for survival. I felt humbled, and at the same time hopeful because of the natural bridges between us – the desire to lead a good life, acts of kindness in unforgiving lives.

★ ☽ ★

Over the next few weeks communications with my family were sporadic. Letters were stalled, phone lines broken, and when we did speak, our conversations were perfunctory. When I could, I would send emails, some recounting small things, others big ones, the unrelenting fortitude of a suffering people. My father's illness had stabilised. As always I worried for him, but the distance had placed me in a bubble of unreality. I had changed. I was detached. I didn't fit in anywhere.

In an alien world I found refuge in friendship, particularly with the women. As the hours and days passed we talked often and freely. It was an incredible privilege to spend time with them. They were generous and spirited, their kindness unlimited. I became somewhat in awe of them. The women of Afghanistan were the strongest I had met. They resigned themselves to the reality that marriage imposed. Behind the high walls of their houses they wept at ambitions never to be realised. They never lost hope. Like the kites, the dreams of the women still flew.

During those days I often visited the school where the children were sad, happy and beautiful. They possessed little more than the clothes they stood up in. Aged beyond their years, they showed an aptitude and an appreciation for learning I could never have imagined. The longer I stayed the more I felt convinced that learning was the key. It was education that would eventually pave the way to peace in Afghanistan, but the process would be a long one.

The English lessons I was giving Ahmed proved an adventure for both of us. He remembered 'gun', 'bread' and 'thank you' with ease, but struggled with any words to do with household arrangements. The more I persisted with his cooking vocabulary, the more deliberately he forgot it.

Often I travelled in Tariq's old sidecar, undercover and unseen in my burka, and when Tariq was off working, as often was the case, I would walk in the old quarter and buy bags of *noqul,* sugar-coated almonds. I copied the gait of the Afghan women, looking down as they did, walking gently and slowly, slipping along the alleys of the old city. Though I sensed they could tell from my feet that I was not one of them, no one stopped or questioned me.

In this way the garment that curbed women's freedom facilitated my own, removing the external differences between myself and the Afghans. I learned for myself how the burka instilled submission in a woman – the lowered head, the limitations that wearing it enforced on the wearer. Imposing it gave men power. Although it was meant to hide the sexual beauty of a woman from men, it succeeded only, as I saw it, in controlling that beauty.

The prison of the burka forced women to walk slowly. It restricted their movement and if they tried running they would fall. Yet many had no choice but to submit to it, just as they submitted to their husbands. As I watched them walking, I imagined their movements as a dance of oppression. It was an ironic image. The Taliban, of course, had banned dancing, according to them a dangerous pastime that encouraged the passions and took the mind off the spiritual. But for the women it was not dancing that was dangerous, but the burka. The garment itself was a tyrant. It taught women to dance with the darkness the veil had inflicted on them.

CHAPTER 8

'Give An Onion Graciously'

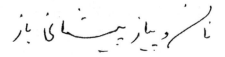

Outside Kabul's orthopaedic centre the crippled waited in long queues, sitting, leaning, hobbling on crutches with crude false legs that didn't fit properly. Some stared into the distance, as if numbed by their pain.

Across the street we waited patiently. We were late, but neither Sohaila and Maryam seemed to be too bothered. Time was always something of a mystery in Afghanistan. Appointments drifted, meal times slipped. Buses had no timetables, arriving and leaving when they felt like it. The only way of mapping a day were the hours of prayer, the muezzin's call the most reliable method of pinning down a point in the anarchy.

The invitation had arrived with the message that the 'foreign lady' was also welcome. Tariq and Ahmed were meeting us there. I felt privileged. I had put on my best scarf and *shalwar khemeez,* and was looking forward to meeting Zaki, having heard so much about him. I wanted to see for myself whether he was good enough for Maryam. Would he take care of her? Did he really want to get married? The jury was out.

The 1960s Mercedes bus announced its arrival with a jangling necklace of metal chains. There were paintings all over the sides – a pair of fishes, a Swiss chalet, an angry tiger, a paradise garden and the words 'Trust in God' emblazoned along the top. Though the front was empty, the back was stuffed with burkas. We made our way down the seats to the section behind the curtain, and squeezed in with the other women, children and shopping bags. As the engine began clonking, someone hopped on, a great beast of an Afghan with a large plastic bag.

'Has anyone got any hashish?' screamed the man. Everyone fell silent. 'Not me!' croaked one, then another of the passengers. He delved into his jacket and whipped out a chunk of hashish the size of a loaf. 'Would anyone like to buy? The best A-grade in Afghanistan!' He looked around searchingly, but with no takers he huffed in disgust and immediately leapt off.

Maryam's hands were shaking, but it was not this man who had caused her face to turn white. She was worried about seeing Zaki again, but at least she was not as scared as she had been when they first met, an occasion she described as the *naamzad bazy*, the 'viewing'. On that occasion she had been so terrified her legs had gone to jelly. Tariq and her uncle had told her to play dumb: it would be too off-putting to appear intelligent. Afghan men did not want intelligent women, women with their own minds. Even if they admired strong women from a distance, they would never marry them. They liked their women silent, obedient, nice and plump, good breeding-stock. They sensed danger when faced with women who might threaten their abilities, preferring to marry someone inexperienced, with only a simple education. In this way they could assume the role of a teacher, and mould their pupil into what they wanted. More often than not, it seemed, the ignorant girl was in hot demand, while the smart, educated and independent one careered towards spinsterhood.

She had expected a much older man, but as she peeked through the doorway, to where her uncle sat with Zaki, drinking tea and smoking cigarettes, she did not think he looked too ancient. Her uncle had introduced them, and she had asked random questions about his family and interests, not delving too deep nor risking exposing her quick intelligence.

Then her uncle had left the room, the door open, leaving them to talk for a while, but watching to ensure there was no physical contact. For a few moments you could have cut the air with a knife. Then, as they began talking, Maryam relaxed a little. She had sensed that he liked her by the way he kept staring at her. She hardly glanced back, since according to tradition she must not make eye contact with her fiancé before the wedding. Although he wasn't exactly her favourite type, his sparkly eyes and bushy black eyebrows added charm to his face, though she couldn't help noticing also his great hooked nose. He had even asked about what she liked and what she didn't, what she enjoyed doing in her spare time, about her teaching job, and whether she would want to continue working after they had married. She decided not to answer that one.

Finally Zaki had come to the most important question: 'How are you at cooking?

'Not bad,' she had said, though in truth she hated it.

Afterwards he had asked her if she had any questions. Maryam had thought hard, then shaken her head. 'No,' she had said. She didn't want to say anything that might put him off. There was a lot riding on it. Men sensed a threat to their authority when they saw a woman being independent. They were afraid because not only did it undermine their manhood but it was an offence against the religious rights of leadership which Allah himself had bestowed on them. She didn't mention continuing to work after they were married. Even if he agreed, he would probably change his mind. If he did not, her teaching would be done in addition, of course, to cooking and looking after the children and the house.

At the end of the meeting, he had told her she was pretty and her cheeks had flushed crimson. She had risen to her feet in a flurry of excuses and had made for the door, heart in her mouth. Since then she had hardly set eyes on him.

★ ☽ ★

Zaki's house lay behind a courtyard shaded by a plane tree. Swallows were darting, unsettled by the noise of the street. They were sensitive souls and the war had had a terrible effect on them. There were a few vestiges of what looked like snapdragons, and a gnarled grapevine entangled on the outside wall, its tendrils like lovers in the dust.

A man with a wizened face smiled gently, his deep lines forming grooves like fissures on an old rock. Tall, with a stoop, and an aquiline nose, Zaki's father greeted us, asking after our health in soft-spoken tones of polite enquiry. He offered us tea and *naan*, and introduced the family; then we all exchanged gifts, just sweets, a cake, scarves, and some biscuits. The ritual of asking after the health continued for some time, the courtesies unfolding like a carpet. It was a ritual I had become not averse to, and it certainly avoided any awkward silences.

Inside the room there were just a few flat mattresses and an oil lamp. The floor was covered with rugs, and on the walls there were framed verses of the Qur'an, a poster of landscapes, and a portrait of Massoud, the Afghan war hero. In the corner a samovar was brewing. Old men sat cross-legged in a circle, as more and more people arrived and squeezed in. Zaki showed us to our places, the men with the men, the women with the children, all the while eyeing Maryam, as she did the same. Ahmed took up the position of honour, away from the door, and Sohaila took the same place in the women's circle.

I felt their eyes on me, how they observed me with good will and scepticism. I ached to blend in, but with no burka to conceal my face I was exposed. I was wrapped in my foreignness. I smelt of it, I breathed it out. It came out of my mouth.

When all twenty of us were seated, a *disterkhan*, a waxed cloth, was spread across the floor and a child brought a bowl and a jug and poured water on our hands. The men were served first. First came the soup, the *sherwa*, which was bones and gravy, mopped up with *naan*; then the rice, sprinkled with rosewater as a finishing touch. They demonstrated the Afghan way, scooping it with skill into a ball, and passing it into the mouth with a flick of the thumb. I tried to do the same and it went everywhere.

The families were young and old and happy and sad, yet the party gave the impression of a unit, bonded in ways that were unspoken because there was no need to speak such things. The men told each other about people they knew who had married, people they had known who had died, and the price and the quality of rice. The women conversed about wedding plans. Everyone had something to say about the corrupt politicians. The Defence Minister owned half of Kabul, they sighed; it was an utter disgrace. The people had no jobs and no future. 'We are dying a slow death,' they said mournfully. God loved Afghanistan. That's why he made its people suffer.

As Zaki spoke softly and intelligently, I warmed to him. He looked modest and mature, with gentle eyes that hinted of his kindness. Like a good Muslim, he prayed to Allah every morning and respected the fast at Ramadan, especially when no one was watching. He wore his tunic below the knee and his trousers below the ankle, just as they should be. His tea was just the right strength, just the right temperature, and not too sweet. He earned less than $100 a month but he was still planning to spend $15,000 on the wedding. He had been saving up for years. No expense was to be spared. It was important to put on a show. The splendour of the occasion ensured that the marriage was accepted. The more elaborate the event, the greater the happiness.

After the meal the families exchanged kisses. I promised to help if there was anything I could do for them. They had shown me such kindness it was the least I could say. As we bade our farewells I thought nothing more of it.

We took up our bags and swished down the road like phantoms. Alongside I glimpsed other burkas rippling in the hot wind, their gauzes no mask against the foul, putrid air. Although today we shared the burka, I felt homesick. I was still a stranger beneath it.

★ ☽ ★

It was late when Tariq dropped me back at the hotel. At the desk lay a lavender envelope, torn at the top, the copperplate writing smudged and distorted. It was only as I picked it up that I saw it had been couriered. I tugged it open and skimmed the lines. I read to the end, then read it again. Four full pages, then a signature and a dozen kisses scratched deep into the blue airmail paper. My mother's words pierced like icicles. My father's cancer had spread.

Head buzzing, heart racing, I rushed back outside and punched out her number. The line was dead. In the silence I caught my breath. I tried once again, and this time it began ringing.

'What's wrong?' I gasped, as she picked up the line.

'Nothing. . .' she said calmly.

'Nothing? How do you mean exactly?'

'There's absolutely nothing you can do here, darling.'

There was a long pause and then nothing, as if the line had been disconnected. I hurried back into the hotel, and threw my things into my suitcase, then booked myself on to the next flight out. Having sluiced my face with some yellowy liquid from the water pipe, I pulled on some socks and struggled into my nightie.

Lying down was useless. I sat up again, shivering, arms

around my knees. Shadows flickered on the ceiling and the walls. As dawn drew closer, the dark patches began moving again, expanding, elongating, darting and contracting. It was quite some time before it occurred to me that the patches were not of my imaginings, but my old friends, the beetles.

After breakfast I said my goodbyes to the family and left in Mr Omar's taxi, my Afghan friends accompanying me to the airport, the traffic at its usual standstill, I locked in my own internal jam. We were all part of Allah's plan, said Tariq as he waved me off. As I climbed on to the plane it felt as if a limb had been severed, but I was powerless to stop it bleeding.

CHAPTER 9

'A Tree Doesn't Move Unless There is a Wind'

صدا از یک دست نمی برآید

In London it was drizzling. Nothing much seemed to have changed except for the faces, which looked sadder and paler than before. My hair, unshielded, felt strange. I tamed it into an unruly knot, twisted it up into position again, clamped it with a comb and forgot it.

Home felt just the same, the familiar stale odour and ugly pictures in the corridors, the eccentric lift, the porter with his cheery smile in the face of abject monotony, the drab front door of my flat. At the same time, everything had changed. I had changed. I had the feel of somewhere else in my speech, my walk, my clothes and my outlook.

I had left Kabul suddenly, overwhelmed by the suffering I had seen, the answers to questions I had gone out with still evading me, now replaced with a whole new batch of equally, if not more, important ones. How could yet another war possibly solve the problems of the Afghans and not exacerbate them? What was needed to help them in a way that was meaningful, which would heal their wounds rather than deepen them, without political or religious agenda? I was as unable to answer any of these ones also. I kept on pondering. Just because questions were hard didn't mean you should stop trying with them.

Fortunately, the deterioration in my father's health turned out to be temporary. An operation to remove the source of the cancer proved successful. The crisis now became largely due to the side effects of the radiotherapy which left his neck red raw and which needing continual dressing. I didn't regret the decision to leave and go back to him. I just blamed myself for having deserted him in the first place. He held up bravely through his pain. Though his voice remained a whisper, his smile had not once faded. It spoke loud of his fortitude. My mother was showing equal courage, but the strain on her had been great and I was glad to be there with her.

We became experts in replacing tubes and cleaning them. The one in his neck helped him breathe more easily, and another bypassed his oesophagus and dripped liquid food directly into his stomach. His face remained swollen, his limbs heavy. Sometimes he felt blind, he said. The link between his senses had been lost and his balance had gone. He felt wasted. He was a waste.

The strangeness I felt in returning home served to sharpen his own sense of estrangement as he found his body not working properly. It no longer felt as if it was his own body, but foreign. It was as if he were being expelled from it because it was sick of him. As the months went by gradually his condition improved, and a short period of remission brought fresh hope.

Newspaper reports spoke of the loss and tragedy in the south of Afghanistan, and like everyone else, I was in awe of the courage and sacrifice of our troops there. Yet I had a different perspective. I had learnt first hand that there were as many stereotypes surrounding foreigners in Afghanistan as Westerners held of Afghans, and that those stereotypes needed to be broken down as much as our own misjudged stereotypes. I questioned the war there more strongly than ever. I knew it had ramifications that went beyond what the newspapers told us, and those issues were complex. They were tribal and historical. The argument that we were there to stem the extremists felt shaky. The root causes of terrorism appeared to have moved on. Now there was resentment borne of a whole new set of issues. Our invasion into Helmand had brought mixed feelings to ordinary Afghans who were angry because our troops killed innocents caught in the crossfire of a war they had never approved of in the first place.

When it came to giving aid, it was equally tricky. Foreigners and Afghans were as divided in their outlook as they were divided by their living arrangements. Many Afghans argued that Westerners made promises they did not keep, that they took their jobs and brought values into their country that were alien and unholy. I feared that in trying to help matters we were only making them worse.

★ ☽ ★

Winter felt a long time coming, and when it did arrive it was long and hard, though it was much longer and harder for the Afghans. Tariq communicated sporadically by email during those months. Sohaila had never used email, so she passed on her news through her daughter. The children suffered badly, she wrote, from the freezing temperatures, from disease, from lack of food and proper clothing. I sent parcels, but felt ashamed. It was not enough, and it never would be.

The security situation had become so bad that foreigners were altogether forbidden to walk alone in Kabul's bazaars. I had been fortunate to have moved so freely, to have escaped without incident. The war was getting worse. More and more innocent civilians were losing their lives and a diplomatic solution seemed farther off than ever.

Maryam wrote. There was a resignation about her emails, not just about the occupation. When she said there was no use fighting it, I knew she also meant her own situation. It would be spring soon and by then she would be a married woman. Zaki had visited once or twice since I had left and though he didn't exactly blow her away she knew it would benefit her family. She had come to the conclusion that he was very kind, but very ordinary. She would not thank Allah every morning waking up beside him. She would not feel her heart beat wildly each time he looked at her. As she gradually confessed her secrets my heart ached for her. I worried for her, for her future and her freedom. I wanted her to be happy, to love and be loved, by someone who deserved her – however impossible that idea might seem.

Secretly I knew Maryam wanted it all, wanted to love her husband with a love that filled her heart forever, a man who was gentle and who cared for her, a marriage rich and strong, children who would be healthy and grow up in a country filled not by war but by peace. She did not dare to dream such things were possible. She knew true love could never be replaced by a run-of-the-mill love, but she would make do, like her mother had done, like all the women in her family before her. She didn't believe in fairy tales.

★ ☽ ★

Several more months passed without further word from Afghanistan. Then one evening everything changed. I was practising the piano when suddenly the phone rang. It rang and stopped, then rang again, but as soon as I answered it the line became disconnected. Half an hour later it went again and this time the line finally held fast. Tariq's voice was agitated. He was garbling, half English, half Farsi, voice peaking with emotion.

'Slow down,' I pleaded. 'You have to speak clearly . . . '

'He's been missing since Friday, *three* whole days . . .'

'Who?' I asked, trying to make sense of it.

'It's Zaki,' he gasped. 'We think he's been kidnapped.'

PART TWO

In a Spin

Chapter 10

'Fate Makes the Mirror Needy of Ashes'

روزگار آسينه را تاج خاکستر کند

As soon as I opened my eyes, I remembered. I made faces in the curtains, but the expressions seemed to jeer and frown. I rubbed away the sleep dust, stretched and dragged myself up, head whirring. In the bathroom cold water splashed on puffy eyes but failed to soothe them. The coffee was sweet, but the plight of my friends stayed bitter. No one had been more generous to me. I recalled a somewhat reluctant cup of tea I was once offered having driven five hundred miles to Scotland to visit someone. Then I thought of my Afghan friends. They possessed nothing, but they had shown kindness and generosity beyond anything I had experienced at home.

I had also given them my word that if anything went wrong I would be the first one to help them, and although promises were tricky, easy to make and difficult to keep, I couldn't ignore it. I didn't know much about life, but there was one thing I was convinced about – I couldn't let them down. I put everything on hold, threw a few things in a suitcase and turned up at Heathrow. This time my family were silent. They knew that it was futile to argue.

★ ☽ ★

It was autumn in Kabul, time of the harvests. A cooling wind swept the Shamali plain, but in Kabul it muddied the air where the usual dirt drifted. Eyebrows and beards turned white with it and the air struggled with its million flecks. Much felt unchanged. Men loitered in doorways as they had always done. Small stoves burned in the shadows at street corners. Armed guards gathered, huddling round a fire or a building, crouching, clasping their rifles.

The traffic was still largely stationary, and the roadblocks just as frustrating, but security had noticeably tightened. Kabul centre now seemed to resemble a fortress. More exclusion zones and roadblocks made it harder to move about. There were more blast barriers round embassies and government buildings, and they were thicker and higher. NATO troops patrolled in full combat gear. There was a sense of malevolence, of despair, and of resignation, though Omar was ever-cheerful as he lamented the state of things. 'It's worse than ever,' he said, slamming the wheel with his fists. 'More dead bodies these days.'

Tariq's house was crammed with relatives. The smiles had gone. The brows were furrowed. Tariq looked wan, his hair dishevelled, his sad eyes bloodshot. Sohaila looked no better as she took my hand in trembling fingers, and Ahmed greeted me like a long-lost daughter. 'Where are my English lessons?' he asked keenly, as if oblivious of the crisis unfolding around him.

Sohaila brought *naan* and Maryam poured tea, her eyes swollen from lack of sleep and crying. I wondered, to begin with, why she was so upset, knowing she had reservations about marrying Zaki. Had she suddenly fallen in love with him while I was away? Only gradually did I realise how naive I was being. Many other factors were at play: the respectability that marriage would bestow on her and her family, the expectations of her mother.

It did not look good. Zaki had not been at work for a week, and no one had seen him for days. Maryam had been bewildered, waiting for his usual call, then waiting until the next day, in vain. It had taken a lot to overcome her resolve not to call him, but when she finally did she found his mobile was switched off. What was going on? Had she done something to upset him? Was he avoiding her? She had tried to call his family, and when eventually she got hold of them, it turned out they were as anxious as she was. They hadn't heard from him in ages.

'Surely someone must have seen something?' I drained my tea glass, wishing for something stronger.

'He was last seen near the zoo, but that was eight whole days ago,' exclaimed Tariq.

'So what are his chances?'

'It depends. If Taliban have him, not good.'

'And do you think they do?' I hardly dared ask the question.

'We don't know . . .'

'Have you rung the police?'

'They're not interested.'

'What can we do?'

'Nothing.'

'I think I need a drink,' I said.

'Here,' said Tariq, pouring out another glass of hot

sweet tea, which wasn't what I had in mind.

'And the ransom?'

'We have no money.' Maryam's voice was hoarse. 'No money, no result. One month; no news, nothing will happen. Three months, dead body. Finish.'

It was unbearable to see her so upset. As she turned her eyes on me, I was overwhelmed by a need to help her. I was not rich by Western standards, but by Afghan ones I was Croesus.

'How much do you need?' I asked tentatively.

'It is impossible to say: one thousand, twenty thousand, fifty,' replied Tariq.

Before I knew it the words were out of my mouth. 'I will try to find it for you,' I said.

They were gazing at me with a mixture of emotions.

'How much do you have already?' piped up Ahmed quickly, unable to disguise the excitement in his voice.

'You should not encourage her,' scolded Sohaila.

'You should not doubt her,' said Maryam, dabbing her eyes on her veil.

I turned out my pockets, and let Ahmed flick through the pitifully thin book of travellers' cheques. 'Is that all?' he said, wrinkling his nose judgementally.

'There's more in the hotel room,' I said brightly.

'I'm not sure,' said Tariq. 'We shall have to do a great deal of thinking . . .'

They gathered round, muttering animatedly. A round of uncomfortable stares followed a reluctant shaking of heads. As they pondered the question further, they stroked their beards in intent concentration before, at last, their heads bobbed unanimously in agreement.

Ahmed's voice rose above the rest. Zaki was a very good man, an honest man, he said, as if the family risked losing a lucrative business deal, which they did. It was an excellent match. They'd be hard pressed to better it.

Eventually they turned to me, thanking me most graciously. It was very generous, they said, but it was not their way. They couldn't possibly accept.

'You could pay me back out of the bride money,' I said. I didn't really mean it. I just said it to make them feel better.

Faces flickered as they considered the proposition. Then slowly something shifted. The old face lit, the young ones cheered, and the little ones squeaked, as their Afghan pride was swallowed. 'Yes, yes, that is an honourable solution,' they sighed at last.

It was a curious form of sophistry, but I regarded it as a victory.

That afternoon we planned like generals. Maps were spread out, notes studiously taken, ideas raised and shot down over quantities of tea and through clouds of cigarette smoke. We would begin by retracing Zaki's steps, visit the zoo, and speak to those he worked with. Until the kidnappers made contact, we would be operating in the dark.

'We have three things on our side,' said Tariq, his eyes on fire. 'One, contacts. Two, hope.'

'And three?'

'Why Allah himself, of course!' There was no way we could fail.

CHAPTER 11

'All that is in the Heart is Written on the Face'

چـــــزنکه دردل است دردهن بُت

Dust lay thick in the morning air, and hung low over the city. The streets felt emptier than usual. At the zoo, there was no perimeter fencing, just a few tawdry buildings huddling wearily in the middle of a roundabout. In the centre of it all a statue of a lion stood bravely at the entrance, as if it could see clearly through the haze that engulfed it.

The script of the sign on the lion's statue was barely discernible as I tried to decipher the letters, only afterwards noticing the English translation. Marjan, the zoo's most celebrated inhabitant, it read, had been a gift from West Germany in the 1960s; he had survived life on the front line for years, but his fortunes had turned when an Afghan fighter broke into his cage in a display of bravado. Marjan responded, as any lion would do, by biting his arm off. The man later died in hospital, and in revenge his brother threw a grenade into the lion's enclosure, blowing off the side of his muzzle, tearing into his legs, and leaving him blind in one eye.

Marjan had died at the grand age of forty-five, of

suspected liver failure. His body had been wrapped in a quilt and laid in a king-sized coffin. His funeral had been worthy of a prince.

I sat on the ground cross-legged. I had abandoned the burka, but even in a veil I was still blind to the impression I was making. It was well known that the zoo was a great favourite of the Taliban, who had allowed it to continue throughout their rule, on the basis that animals were the creatures of Allah. A caring side to the Taliban? The thought was surprising. When it came to humans their cruelty was legendary, destroying anything that was enjoyable in life.

Tariq was running late again. He'd be just five minutes, he had said, which meant more like fifteen. Predictably, five minutes turned into ten and soon became fifteen. I waited, checking my watch from time to time, clutching my phone. I glanced around idly, noticing the mud on the building and the smoothness of its surfaces as, in the corner of my eye, the mud flickered.

A shape became clearly identifiable. At first I thought it was some rags, a bird maybe, or a cat. I looked again and the shape moved sideways. It was only at that moment that I saw it properly. It was a dog, mangy and emaciated. Sand-flies buzzed about its muzzle but it appeared not to notice them. It was difficult to make out what kind of dog it was, with its pale, muddy fur, pointed ears, and narrow muzzle, or even whether it was a bitch or a dog; but what was clear was its starving thinness. Nothing unusual about that – there were many such dogs in the city, all unloved, running wild in packs and terrifying people. Yet this one seemed somehow different. I fancied it was one I had seen before. Then again, it was not unlike the many others that roamed the streets here. Surely I was mistaken. After all, I usually was.

I bent down to take a closer look, but it was already too late. Scared by my phone, which had woken and was singing like a sparrow, the dog had shot off. I pressed the button and listened. Tariq's voice was excited.

'I've just spoken to the police . . . they think we would know if he'd been taken by the Taliban.'

'So is that good news?'

'It's not bad.'

We chatted briefly and I promised him I would wait for him. His parting instruction was clear.

'Don't try to pick any flowers or they'll blow your arm off . . .'

'But Tariq . . .' I said, glancing around at the rubble and dirt, 'there aren't any.'

I bought a ticket and wandered in with the crowd. Men and women sat on plastic chairs at plastic tables and eyed each other cautiously. A keeper was sweeping the dust with a broom, kicking it up into the air and letting it fall again in almost exactly the same spot. But it was not the keeper who made me start, nor Tariq's rushing shadow approaching behind me. With so much human suffering, it seemed everyone had forgotten the fate of the animals.

It was a sight that sickened me. Two mangy wolves sat limply, one chewing a piece of cardboard; a brown bear paced agitatedly, his nose bloody and infected; a couple of baboons looked out vacantly, one nibbling on a cigarette stub across a moat of putrid, foul-smelling water. An elderly man with Mongol features was peering intently into a cage of motionless owls and flapping his hat directly in the face of one of them, but it didn't respond. He unwrapped a toffee and threw the wrapper into the cage, inciting a slow, uninterested blink.

A cartoon nailed to one of the cages depicted animals making funny faces at a *homo sapiens* sleeping in a cage, but I wasn't laughing. I was angry. I wanted to save them, but I was powerless. When it came to the dictates of Islam that decreed kindness to all God's creatures, people came first; it was their suffering that counted. I looked away, unable to conceal my sadness or force a smile.

A keeper leant on a bristly broom. As he stroked his beard, his face said it all: sadness, memory, silence and ruin. I didn't need the Dari. Tariq translated but I gazed through the bars, hardly hearing him. He had put up a sign, he said: 'Dear citizens, the animals are creatures of Allah. While watching them, please avoid annoying or bothering them.' But everyone ignored it. 'The problem is not with the animals,' he said slowly so I could understand him better, 'it's the people. They pelt them with stones, sticks, shoes and even their hats, and kill them by feeding them chewing-tobacco.'

His stories were hair-raising. Once a man had climbed into the wolves' cage and attacked one of the males with a brick, leaving him deaf and blind in one eye. Many of the animals were dying of starvation, and those that survived were often eaten out of necessity. That was apart from the wild boar, who survived because of the Islamic ban on pork.

Others, such as Hathi, the twenty-five-year-old elephant, had fallen victim to rocket fire. During the freezing winter months, the keepers often took the birds home at night, he said. They begged for food for the animals at the bazaar, relying on the good will of the local butcher who gave meat for the animals, though sometimes the keepers used it to feed their families instead. Income from tickets went to the state, and none of the staff had been paid for months. He stayed because he cared for the animals, and because of his faith. Usually he made $20 a month, which was barely enough to feed his seven children. He had to sell his clothes, and even then they had been hungry.

There was no good moment to speak of our own dilemma, but Tariq was determined. He pulled the photo of Zaki from his pocket and showed it to the keeper.

'Her husband?' asked the keeper, glancing at me furtively.

'No,' said Tariq, 'my sister is engaged to him.'

The keeper looked perplexed. He was considering the matter most carefully. No, he said gravely, he certainly had not seen this man. He was very handsome . . . kind eyes . . . he would have remembered him. I handed him some dollars. As his fingers tightened over the bundle of notes, a tear trickled slowly down his deeply lined cheek. His tone appeared to change slightly. Tariq grew excited. He was talking animatedly in a dialect that was beyond me, begging me to write something. I plucked the paper out of my bag and began scribbling: Zibagul. To me it meant nothing. No, said Tariq, as he set off to pick up the sidecar, it was a lead.

I stood by the entrance, unable to stop shaking. A bush by the roadside seemed to shake in reflection. It seemed the shrubbery was hiding something. The undergrowth shivered slightly. Something moved. A paw stuck out, then another, until finally the whole had emerged from its camouflage. I saw immediately it was a she-dog.

The raspberry creams from my bag broke easily into pieces. They were half smashed anyway. I placed them down and stepped back. The tail gave a flick before drooping pathetically. The dog kept her distance, settling down on all fours, legs tucked under. Then she rolled on her back in what I imagined to be a submissive gesture.

I called to her softly and tried to let my voice rise slightly, moving forwards a little. But it was too much. The dog drew away with the faintest whimper. It sat down again, panting. We stayed for a few minutes in this position, neither of us moving much, oblivious to the traffic that roared past on the road. Finally, just as I was about to give up and go, she rose, lolloped over and began wolfing down the biscuits.

I crouched down to take a closer look. There was something almost lupine in the chiselled face, the curve of the jaw. The fur was thick, but the condition was poor. On the neck an open sore bled, the left hind paw had a swelling, the ears were full of ticks, and in the mouth blood mixed with saliva.

She finished the biscuits and turned her dark eyes on me. Then she cocked her head, brushed against me and sniffed, inhaling deeply. I moved my hand nearer to her nose to let her smell it, praying she wouldn't bite it. I need not have feared. She just sniffed at it softly, as if the hand were made of porcelain.

It was almost too painful to think how her life must have become a long struggle for survival, rummaging through foul-smelling rubbish for scraps. I imagined her as a puppy, tail upright, brave and playful, though the reality must have been a far cry from the pictures in my head. Abuse, starvation and neglect – I dreaded to think what experiences she had suffered around humans in her short life. Though free to roam the streets, like the animals in the zoo, she was locked in a cage from which she could not escape, a prison of despair.

I sat down in the dirt, distracted. I had often read the stories of dogs rescued in these parts, the ones that always ended in tears. It could only end badly. With a leaden heart I put down the rest of the biscuits, and buried my face in my hands as the sidecar came spluttering to a halt beside us. 'Forget it!' came the voice from the driving-seat.

'Surely we can do *something* . . .' I whined, but as the engine began revving, the noise was too much. The dog started and limped off. I squeezed into the seat, we pulled away, and I watched her, until she became smaller and smaller, like a dot in a Seurat painting.

CHAPTER 12

'Smell of Perfume Comes from the First Deal'

سودای اول بوی مشک است

Muffled voices echoed, amid a few sharp bangs. Tariq went outside to see what the commotion was while we waited, breath bated, inside the house. Moments later he bounced back in, and he was not alone. They were friends, he said with a flourish, as two small men, wiry as meerkats, shuffled in silently. Behind them ambled a bear of a man, loud and unruly. My jaw dropped. My eyes widened. He reminded me of someone, with that curly black beard, those hairy fingers. I considered for a moment, before suddenly it struck me. Goddammit, it was Blackbeard the Pirate.

Blackbeard flashed a thumbs-up sign and beamed, front tooth twinkling like a lone star. He had fought with the Mujahedin, he said in his loud, deep voice, 'those who struggled'. He described them as warriors of Islam, divided by their tribes but united in their love for their country and dedication to honour, to Allah and, most important of all, to freedom. No sooner had he roared his unpro-nounceable name, than I forgot it. I decided to christen him Genghis. Well, he did say he was a warrior.

The men slung down their guns and squatted. The two

small men silently stared at me, while the large one began expounding, lighting up his roll-up cigarette and puffing imperiously. Tariq translated the hard sentences, which equated to virtually all of them. If we wanted to get this person back, it would take time, patience and perseverance. Even then the problems were immense and unfathomable.

Bakshishi was a word used in many sentences. Many palms would need greasing. It was a good thing I was rich. We would have to negotiate between the Afghan army and the US military and the Taliban. If we kept a low profile, the kidnappers would see Zaki wasn't important and might release him. If we looked too keen, we might invite impossible conditions for his release and an even higher ransom. Even if we could discover where he was being held, three out of the four main roads out of the city were controlled by the Taliban, and much of the area was out of the question because of Islamist insurgents. After all that, he might already be dead.

We all fell silent for a moment, which meant no difference at all for the two small men, who had said nothing at all anyway. Tariq, however, who had for some time been trying to get a word in edgeways, had an efficient air about him as he set about relating what the zookeeper had told us.

Zibagul, echoed Genghis, smoothing down his beard, was an opium farmer, a dealer and an old hand well known to the authorities. Zibagul lived in Panjshir. It was a long shot, but in the circumstances, since we had no shots, any shot would do.

'Well, we should go there at once . . .' As the words fell from my mouth I failed to consider the impact they were having on the others.

'*We* should go there?'

'Yes,' I said. 'I would like to come with you . . .'

The uncomfortable stares began, followed by the head-shaking and beard-stroking. While I pointed out the 'ifs', Tariq supplied the 'buts', forgetting his manners and using his left hand to wipe the grease of the cheese off his chin. How could we dodge the authorities, keep a low profile, and avoid word getting out to the Taliban that a lone foreign woman was with them? Make one mistake, and we would all be dead.

'I wouldn't want to put anyone else in danger . . .' I said.

'You wouldn't be doing that,' said Genghis nobly, but we all knew it was a lie.

It was a tricky dilemma. On the one hand, if I was funding the bribes, I wanted to make sure the money went into the right hands. At least that was the excuse I gave now. Underneath, something else had short-circuited my fear and it wasn't just the death wish. In truth I wanted to face myself. I thought if could test myself, drive myself to the limit of my abilities I might learn something, of the past, and of where I had gone wrong. It felt somehow that it was only in these outer limits of my comfort zone, with everything stripped back, that the questions from my past which haunted me might be answered. Above all else, someone was in danger and I wanted to save him. All that was fair enough, but if it was going to put other people's lives at risks, obviously it was a non-starter. That, quite simply, would be reckless.

Tariq rubbed his hair, teasing it until the crown of his head was standing up like a tuft of feathers. Shrugging his shoulders, he listed their objections. I was a woman. I was a *kafir*. And I was British. It couldn't get any worse.

'What sort of a woman goes gallivanting around a country without a husband, without her family, anyway?' interrupted Ahmed, who was absolutely gobsmacked at the suggestion.

'A foreign one,' responded Genghis matter-of-factly, at which there was a unanimous round of nodding.

'And what sort of man allows her to do such a thing?'

'A stupid one,' growled Genghis wryly, to which answer another round of even more fervent nodding ensued.

'It would be a pity if you died, a waste of good breeding-stock,' said the old man, toying with his braces.

'Yes, indeed!' cried everyone simultaneously.

'*Amniyat nist,* it's not safe,' blurted out Maryam, who up to now had restrained herself.

'You mean for a woman?'

'Exactly,' said her brother, as if he had won the argument hands down.

Sohaila took my hand. 'He is only worried about you,' she said gently, 'as we all are.'

Tariq was shaking his head again. The journey would be arduous. I would be a honey-pot for all the evil that lurked in the shadows. It would be boiling by day and freezing at night. The phones would not work. The roads were bad, and there would be fords and rough stretches, some off bounds to foreigners altogether. The terrain made policing virtually impossible. The dangers were unseen, the muggings and ambushes unpredictable. The threat was real: there were spies everywhere.

Next it was Genghis's turn. He peered at me closely, his dark eyes narrowing, then glanced away. It was the mines he was really worried about. They were the work of the devil. Those IEDs were everywhere. You didn't even have to touch one for it to go off. It could be detonated by remote control, even by a mobile phone. Then there were those evil little UXOs. There were two types, one specially for tanks, the other for people; these lay in wait for unsuspecting hands exploring in the rubble or in ruined buildings. Then there were the bright yellow ones. The Russians really hated those. Or the little airborne ones, the PFMs and PMSs that fluttered down from Soviet war planes like butterflies. Pretty. Deadly. They looked like toys, so were a favourite with children.

Having avoided direct eye contact, he glanced furtively back at my paling face. Even worse than those, he continued, waggling a hairy forefinger at me, were the POMs. Those were titchy discs on small wooden sticks that always fell off when disturbed, blasting everything in sight. And they were cunning, too, with plastic pellets instead of metal, and harder to find in a body. Even more evil than all those were the jumping mines, which leapt up before exploding. 'Boomb!' They were snared, with trip wires often connected to bigger networks. Sometimes they were attached to something deliberately meant to draw the curiosity of a passer-by.

'Just like the flowers,' I said hoarsely.

'Exactly!' echoed the men in chorus, as if I had really hit on something.

On the plus side, added Genghis more lightly, clocking the fear now writ large across my face, they knew all the secret routes and could introduce us to the villagers.

Tariq stood up suddenly, pacing about like an agitated

general. 'I've had an idea,' he said, glancing at Genghis. Genghis glanced back, and the pair began whispering. The two small staring men grinned knowingly.

I waited, all ears.

'You must disguise yourself,' said Tariq. As a foreigner, I stuck out like a watermelon in a rice field. I must go literally undercover, I must put on the burka. It was our only chance to ensure everyone's safety. The guards at the checkpoints would never ask an Afghan woman to lift the veil. He was sure we'd get away with it.

Genghis looked puzzled. It would be an interesting experiment, he said, but the disguise had to be convincing. My skin was too white. I must dye my arms dark. Even on the apparently safe roads I must hide my face completely. I must under no circumstances wander off, or we'd all be done for.

'Oh, I have no intention of doing that,' I said, still recovering from the idea.

'But can you lie low?' Tariq was looking decidedly wary.

I nodded vaguely.

They whispered again animatedly. When we approached checkpoints I would have to stay quiet. I would have to do as I was told.

I looked at them dubiously. They had no idea how much they were asking.

'Are you sure you want to?' Genghis's whiskers were rippling visibly.

'Yes, Genghis,' I said, still not really thinking it through.

'*Jheengheeez?*' he bellowed, whiskers still quivering.

'On condition you will not be risking your lives for

me. I wouldn't want to jeopardise the mission or to put you in danger . . .'

'*Khoob*,' he huffed, ignoring me, 'but you are *never* to call me *Jheengheez* again!'

Tariq was equally selfless. 'You are not aid worker. You are not journalist. You are not missionary. If worst comes to worst we will say we are saving you.'

'From what?'

'Why from yourself, of course,' they said curtly.

Against everyone's better judgement a route was agreed, a deal settled, and a plan hatched, though I didn't believe them for a minute when they said it was foolproof. Genghis was team leader and Tariq translator. The two small staring men, who turned out to be Genghis's nephews, were also coming, though I wasn't exactly sure what their role was. I would be wearing Maryam's burka, wearing Maryam's trousers. In case of an emergency I would be taking Maryam's documents.

Uncertain as I was at the thought of placing myself in the hands of such an unlikely crew of bodyguards, I forced myself into an uneasy calm. Only Allah knew the answers, and, when it boiled down to it, he was Tariq's best contact of all.

★ ☽ ★

Three days later we were ready. Supplies had been bought and the journey arranged. Genghis's jeep was a war trophy. He had captured it from the Soviets, and twenty years later it was still going strong. At least, that was his story. When the time came to get in, something held me back. Perhaps it was the cloud of smoke issuing from the exhaust. It might have been the fact that the rear-view mirror was missing, or the loud screech of brakes as it edged up beside me. Then again, it might have been the uncertain nature of the upholstery, or indeed the lack of it, for the stiff, hard seats were devoid of padding. But what took the biscuit was the absence of glass altogether in some of the windows. Only after gentle coaxing failed to have an effect did Tariq push me in.

I braced myself for a difficult journey. I had sent a handwritten note to the British Consulate to let them know I was going and had signed it with an illegible scribble. They would only have tried to talk me out of it. As Maryam and Sohaila waved goodbye I wished they were coming with us, but nothing on God's earth could persuade them to change their minds.

The men seemed to have no luggage at all, just a few tins, a couple of wonky candles and a dusty copy of the Qur'an. Nothing could beat the perfect, timeless and unchanging word of Allah, Tariq said reverently, as if Allah himself were listening. It was a one-stop shop of rules and prescriptions, a moral compass. It was just as important as the guns, he said, which was saying something.

Of course, the question as to whether I should take my own weapon had been greeted with even more beard-stroking and frowning than usual, especially after I had confessed that all I knew about guns was that there was a long one called a rifle, a short one called a pistol, and a fat one called a cannon. I had only myself to blame for the pathetic Swiss Army penknife they allocated to me.

The food supplies were equally questionable. Word had

it the goods on sale at the Bush Bazaar had been gleaned from the US and British military bases, but judging by the sell-by dates on the ready-made meals, they had probably already been thrown out. It was a good thing the men were travelling light, since I myself had a small convoy of bags. Genghis had prised the large one with toiletries out of my hands, but I had clung on with terrier tenacity to the loo paper, refusing to give it up for all of England.

'I knew you were going to be a handful,' he said. To soothe him, I admired his beard, and he softened, his nose wrinkling bashfully. He washed it with rosewater, brushed it, smoothed it down every morning, combed it like the Prophet, forty times on the front and the same on the underside, but he never trimmed it. 'The beard should be allowed to run free in the wind,' he said. It was said to increase a man's vivacity and intelligence, and, it was claimed, even calm him. 'Above all,' he assured me, 'it is a sign of intelligence – after all, it is in the *hadeeth*!'

'Ah, that explains it,' I said, smiling.

The wheels spun, billowing circles of dust. Tariq sat in the back with Genghis's nephews, who said nothing as usual. Genghis entered into battle with the steering wheel and we were off, the tarpaulin roof flapping in time with my racing heart and my fluttering burka.

Away from the pollution of the city, the air cleared. As each checkpoint approached I froze with fear, but not one soldier lifted an eyebrow. To the surprise of all of us, the plan appeared to be working. The heat was blistering. I looked like a nun and felt like a pizza oven. My veil was glued to my head with perspiration and the Evian spray I kept squirting at my face. Sometimes I lifted my visor, and the warm breeze felt sweet against my cheek as at last I could see properly.

It was a landscape of beauty mingled with war scrap. There were groves of mulberry, cherry, apricot and almond trees. Villagers chatted animatedly around stalls bursting with grapes of green and purple. Irises and gentians flourished in ancient rubber tyres. Around them husks of tanks lay rusting like upturned turtles, and craters were strewn with metal. Mud structures half destroyed by shells peppered the hillsides. Unexploded bombs lay openly in their casings at the roadsides. Mud-brick cubes seemed to rise from the land as if struggling to break free of it. Sometimes a very different kind of building eclipsed them. Tariq called them poppy palaces. Pink and red, gaudy and showy, they stood along the ancient silk route. Today there were no exotic caravans laden with precious silks and spices. Toyota Hilux trucks bore heavies guarding a somewhat different but equally precious cargo – opium.

Tariq and the others were snoring. Genghis drove erratically, one hand on the steering wheel, the other gesticulating, his observations as endless as the twisting, winding scenery. He spoke of freedom and liberation, invasion and occupation, hatred and revenge, of drug-trafficking, cargo-smuggling and the pocketing of international-aid funds that fuelled a trade in luxury goods and high-tech communications.

'Why is everyone so suspicious of foreigners?' I asked him.

'We know you leave your families and put yourselves in danger to help us, but why insult our culture while you are at it?' he said. 'It takes less than a minute to destroy a house, but to rebuild it takes a lifetime.' As he spoke, I couldn't help wondering if it was the same for people.

Normally, he was a shepherd, he said. He slept rough under the stars, washed in the springs, and lived off the land. There were about 650 sheep, watched by a dozen shepherds, and he earned a tenth of each year's lambs. As well as his guns he owned an ox, a plough, and a cow, but that was about it. Everything else was lost to him now: his wife, his parents, his children. All had died in the wars.

As I struggled to comfort him, my pathetic Farsi was not helping matters. Love would always be hard, painful, unpredictable, but in the end, life was nothing without it. According to Socrates, I said, as if intellectualising it might soothe him, there were three kinds of love. First came the state of being in love, of making the object of love more perfect by placing it on a pedestal and gazing at it with awe. This led to the next form of love, the gratification of sensual, unguarded passion. Last of all came 'familiarity mingled with mortal prudence', which was not true love.

Genghis winked knowingly. He had never heard of Socrates, he said, but that last one he knew well. It was the basis of marriage.

No amount of academic analysis could explain true love, of course. True love, said Socrates, was as rare as it was selfless, of the highest nature, rooted not in the senses, nor in the emotional nature, but in a person's will. Often you had to lose it before you understood it, added Genghis. A hairy banana finger rose to his face, wiping a tear from his eye as if swishing a fly.

I warmed to him then, the drooping nose, the ascending moustache, the forest of a beard. This bear had the heart of a lion.

★ ☽ ★

A town loomed and the road widened. To the right lay two bare hills, one with a great white streak down its side made of moving sand. Further ahead stood a village, Pul-e-Mattack, where mounds of snuff or *naswar* were sold in plastic bags. At least that was what I thought it was, but as Genghis smiled wryly I had to wonder. It was at least an hour before we turned right. At Jabal-e Seraj the road twisted downwards. A rocky cliff hung over crystal-clear rapids and a high gorge. Below lay a valley. There were groves of walnut and mulberry trees. Meadows enfolded villages, and maize was spread out on the flat roofs to dry. In the shallows turquoise ducks and waders fed contentedly. All seemed oblivious of unseen dangers, of the snipers, the mines, the bandits.

Another convoy passed by, this time of rocket-launchers. 'Targets for suicide bombers: if you get too close they shoot at you,' winked Genghis, at which I paled and swallowed. The convoy turned off on to a wide paved road which turned out to be part of Bagram, the US army base. The valley fanned out. Fertile land alternated with barren hillsides. Sweeping, undulating lines of ridges and hollows became well-watered meadows. People walked in groups by the roadside, Tajiks with almond-shaped faces, nomads selling goat's cheese and animal skins. Shepherds drove their sheep, distant freckles on the horizon.

We turned off into a track, and the bumping and jerking finally stirred the others. The men swapped drivers, and Genghis squeezed in the back, boots sticking out of the window for airing. The track wound on. Soon a few huts rose out of the dust. In the deserted square lay a pond, a bush, and a well. Poppy fields were never visible from the road or highway. Occasionally, a stray seed or two borne on the wind put an errant flower in a gutter, but that was about it. A few old men were squatting by the side of the road, observing with curiosity and scepticism. Another rode a girl's bicycle with his knees sticking out. Seeing us wave, he stopped the wheels with his heels.

Genghis did the talking, and the rest of us stood behind him. He peered at the old man searchingly, and after the usual courtesies asked him if he knew the famous poppy trader who lived around these parts. 'We don't grow poppy here,' protested the man, wrinkling his skin of nut-brown leather.

'We were told you've just harvested two hundred kilos?'

A flicker of recognition descended across the worn features and suddenly everyone fell about laughing, the flow of Dari rapid and excited. A name was given, an exchange of bank notes, and an explosion of nods and grunts.

We took to the jeep again and drove – past hamlets where babies wore hats with tufted topknots and dangling silver ornaments, past a mud-walled mosque open to the elements where men prayed fervently, towards fields of vegetables and maize, and hillsides where pine nuts grew wild. From the back seat, Genghis buzzed like a great old bee, wafting the rose-water after-shave he had been liberally splashing on the damp patches beneath his armpits. Poppy-growing ran deep in Afghanistan. It was the best of all crops: it needed hardly any water, it paid for weddings and funerals. For many farmers, it was the only lifeline. Everyone knew the drugs mafia controlled government. There were many ways to poison the West. Heroin drove both sides of the civil war between the Taliban and the government. It made the government rich and the Taliban richer. Above all, it funded terrorism.

The road twisted on, up hills and down them again, sometimes so rutted it wrenched the spine, past meadows so soft they looked like velvet. The landscape grew bleaker. There were mixed tribes in this valley, said Tariq, inbred people. The children had strange faces and clubbed feet. They were not his people, the Pashtun. If the tribes varied, the villages looked identical: another cluster of mud roofs, another well, another square, and then another. And then a curve – and there it was at last: a field of pink like a scene from a retro Cadbury's chocolate-flake advert. I wanted to run barefoot, spread my fingers through the leaves, and put my nose to the centres. Then Tariq reminded me the fields were full of mines. One step, and I'd be dead.

Fortunately the house we were looking for was not far. It stood at the side of the field, with ruined walls and a lifeless front, no windows and a sad-looking door, which squeaked as the boy opened it. Inside, the faint glow of a candle threw distortions of shade on the walls. Children crawled over shabby cushions. In one corner a woman crouched like a faded spectre. She might have been fifty, but had piercing eyes and a fiery air. She bore a lovely name that seemed to shine in the gloom and lighten it. It was Zibagul.

CHAPTER 13

'Goat is Hanging from its Own Leg and Sheep from its Own'

نرمه پای خود آویزان است او گوسفند به پای خور

Zibagul poured tea, her fingers twisted with arthritis, her voice as worn as the clothes that hung around her frame. I sipped the fragrant mixture, eyes watering, and a telling look from Genghis revealed that it contained the magic ingredient I suspected. Like the desert snakes, opium had bite. So did the room, it appeared, which was stacked high with opium in plastic yellow packages, some sealed tightly, some bursting at their seams, others oozing a sticky brown substance which Genghis later informed me was opium resin. On the basis that just a kilo of opium was worth £40,000 on the streets of London, this room alone was worth millions.

Zibagul described how her boys carried packs of heroin across the borders because they were poor and had no other way of making a living. They worked cleverly, hiding the bags under the bellies of sheep, even strapping false testicles on to male goats and hiding them in the centre of their herds. They risked their futures every day to smuggle the cargoes. If they were caught, they faced fifteen years in prison and a fine of £25,000. If they were shot, the police wouldn't even let their families take the bodies to bury them. It was all the fault of the government and the foreigners, who only made it worse. Fortunately she had powerful friends, she boasted. There were even Americans involved. One was an influential player in these parts. She couldn't give his proper name, but they knew him as White Ibrahim.

As Tariq translated the Pashto, something distracted us suddenly. A child wandered in, crying and disorientated. She couldn't have been more than five years old, but she needed her fix. In a country where doctors were rare, where children were crippled by indiscriminate bombings, and where painkillers were costly, it was well known that parents gave opium to children to relieve pain because it was cheap and available. It was not surprising they soon became addicted.

'I know what you are thinking,' said Zibagul coldly, reaching for the little one and comforting her. 'I defy anyone to argue. I can show them my barefoot orphan grandchildren.'

'I would not dream of judging you,' I said.

I dug deep into my bag, fished out some packets of antibiotics and placed them on the carpet. It was a pathetic gesture, but I did it anyway.

'Is that all?' she said faintly.

'There might be more,' said Genghis. 'It all depends on the Uzbek man.'

'The Uzbek man?' echoed the old lady, frowning suddenly.

'Yes,' nodded Genghis.

The face darkened, the brow contracted.

'We were told that you knew something?' said Genghis.

'How much have you got?' she snapped.

'How much will it take?' replied Genghis.

'One thousand.'

'*Afghanis*?'

'Dollars.'

'One thousand dollars!' exclaimed Genghis, the hairs of his beard rippling across his chest like serpents.

Tariq took a picture of Zaki and placed it in front of Zibagul. She ignored it. The more Genghis pressed, the more flustered she became. Tariq motioned him to back down and relax. We united in a confirmatory murmur. It was obvious that she was only after the money, thought Tariq. Genghis agreed. I rose to my feet and ran for the door, the men behind me, knuckles whitening round the stocks of their rifles.

We climbed into the jeep, where the nephews were waiting, Tariq sweating with frustration as he fumbled for the ignition, Genghis unlocking his rifle. I fixed my attention on the black stripe of the tarmac, focusing hard as it gleamed against the surrounding yellow expanse. Perhaps it was the speed of Tariq's driving that made everything blurry. The men were convinced it was the tea, although they themselves remained unaffected. They were so used to the stuff they'd become hardened to it.

★ ☽ ★

It must have been several hours before finally something appeared to break the tedium, as in the haze ahead rose a few dark patches. As we rumbled along through this unending landscape I had hardly noticed the time passing, the heat, and the flies. The nothingness of the plain felt like the nothingness of frustration we were all feeling.

The brickworks in the plain looked like ancient temples. Vineyards once stretched out here, but destruction fell on both nature and people in these parts. The Taliban eradicated the Tajiks and left infertile fields and dilapidated irrigation systems. Today the land was just a wilderness, an absence of everything, except a few solitary shapes in the distance. As we drew nearer the shapes began crystallising. I made out turbans, armed figures, military jackets, and ammunition belts. I scrabbled to pull down my burka. Too late. The headscarf would have to do. We drew do a halt and Tariq began negotiating, his voice rising, climbing and peaking in crescendo. As the garbled sentences evaded me, I sensed a dull light cross hardened faces as one asked to see our papers. Was I tripping? He couldn't be a soldier. He looked about nine years old.

When we climbed from the jeep, everything seemed to fade. Genghis and his nephews had gone, and the boy was standing beside me. There was no point in arguing. You wouldn't want to upset the lad. He had a very big gun.

That gun was the last thing I remembered. When I opened my eyes I was on the ground, head throbbing, green spots darting. Figures seemed to disintegrate, multiply and twist into geometric patterns. As I came to my senses a rush of fear, the sort that rolls out of the sky from nowhere, flooded me. I lifted my head and tried to focus, and in the haze of dust the dissolving parts seemed to melt, to merge and sway, and then come together again to form a somewhat familiar whole, a vision not quite real, like a zoetrope. As it steadied, I was comforted to see Genghis's whiskers and hear Tariq's voice, though at first I struggled to understand exactly what they were saying. The soldiers were friendly, they insisted. I had fainted. They suspected it had been the tea.

Some way to the right, the boy was having his photograph taken in front of his BM-21 rocket launcher – with a camera that appeared to be mine. The boy strode over. He seemed a lot less frightening now he wasn't carrying a gun. Even still, as I placed my hand on my heart in greeting I felt it racing. He ushered us towards the broken walls of a mud building. Guards stood at the entrance. They looked about ten years old, but they were wearing guns big and powerful enough for full-grown men. One was staring at me wildly, while the other painted his eyes with kohl, with the aid of a small hand mirror. There were several chambers, a main one for sitting and sleeping in, one for the horses and donkeys, one for Katyusha rockets, and one at the back that stank. I didn't look too closely at that one.

In the main room more boys and some small children sat cross-legged around the smokestack, their Russian AK-47s decorated with pretty beads and wild-rose designs. An oil lamp smoked, but it didn't stop their unblinking gazing at a woman in their presence.

Tariq obliged with a translation of the Pashto. Humayun, it transpired, was about eighteen years old. He was not just a boy; he was a warlord. He had inherited six tanks, an army of three hundred soldiers, and a fiefdom of twenty-six villages. He had first fought on the front line with his father when he was just thirteen, he said, but nowadays that was old. Normally boys began at five. The national army was their vocation, but they found it boring. Taliban soldiers, desperate for new recruits, had visited the local mosques and schools to press-gang teenagers into joining them, offering more money than anyone else could match. But the boys were against a terrorist regime. They thought of themselves as crusaders, prepared to die if necessary in the fight against the Taliban. One boy had escaped with the intention of enlisting in the Afghan national army, aided by guides who knew the tracks through poppy-fields laced with mines. He had been having a maths lesson when three pick-up trucks suddenly roared into the school playground. Armed men had leapt out, pushing the teacher out of the way and brandishing their weapons. 'Who wants to do *jihad* against the British and Americans?' they had shouted.

Jihad. As the word popped out of the Pashto, I jumped. So much fuss about a word that didn't even appear in the Qur'an. I could tell you what the textbooks said – that the word itself was derived from the Arabic root *j-h-d*, meaning effort or striving; that there was a greater and lesser form of it; that in the true sense of the word it meant the battle every person fought in their own heart against their baser nature; that military *jihad* did not refer exclusively to fighting a holy war. But I still didn't understand. Thankfully the Qur'an was clear. In the end the most virtuous path was forgiveness. It was up to Allah to judge who had been wronged and who had wronged whom. *Jihad* was a duty of Islam, but forgiveness was the key.

Humayun ignored the scared expression on my face. As he offered me tea, I couldn't help but wonder what was in it. 'Wait, I'll drink first. Then you have nothing to fear,' he said.

'Thank you,' I replied, and let him drink first before sipping it warily.

He didn't want to join the Taliban, he said. They had shot his father, Aghagan. But he knew why people supported them. He himself had bigger ideas. One day he would like to be president of Afghanistan and put it all right. He wanted to improve his command of English because he wished to study in London. Would I teach him? Would his armed bodyguard cause a stir in classes?

We talked some more, until the light began failing. Humayun stood up, slinging his large gun over his small shoulder. 'You are free to go,' he said casually. Relieved and exhausted, we weren't about to argue. As we turned hurriedly towards the jeep, no one stood in our way. Genghis slammed his foot on the accelerator and we took off in a swirl of dust and diesel, the jeep going into a wild, lurching skid along the broken surface of the road.

'It's all right, they're firing in the air!' cried Tariq reassuringly as a crackle of shots broke out behind us. Genghis wasn't listening. He was concentrating intently, driving the engine to levels untried for a vehicle whose maximum speed had never reached above forty miles an hour.

Only when we had reached Kabul did Tariq confide the truth about the fainting episode. Though he couldn't be sure, he thought one of the soldiers might have struck me from behind. It would have been accidental, of course, he insisted, but in any case we had been very lucky. He hadn't mentioned it at the time because he didn't want to scare me. As he told me I nodded. I wasn't surprised by what he had said and from then on I simply pretended it hadn't happened. It was an act of delusion. Scientists might have called it latent inhibition, the ability to ignore our surroundings and focus. Psychoanalysts might have described it as a coping strategy. But there was more to the thought than sheer bloody-mindedness. In the twisted logic of my irrational thought process, my father was counting on me. I couldn't let him down, and I couldn't let myself down either.

I wrote to let my parents know I was fine. At the post office the options were snail mail, or DHL. It was the shortest letter I had ever sent, as well as being the most expensive.

CHAPTER 14

'A Lion at Home, and a Fox Abroad'

شـــر خانـﻪ و روبا بيرون

The men were busy. Genghis was polishing the mother-of-pearl inlay in the barrel of his gun. It was the love of his life, he said, spitting on it again. Ahmed had been negotiating the small shrubbery of aerials around the television set. His passion for watching was, however, as intense as it was unrequited, so often and so hard would he try in vain to get it to work. This occasion was no different, and the grainy fuzz persisted. Tariq, meanwhile, was pacing again, ear glued to his favourite mobile. That wasn't working either. So he delved into his pocket, drew out another one, and began calling upon the extensive list of his family members – all of whom, it seemed, were out. Exhausted and depleted, he slumped down on the floor.

'We shouldn't have gone there,' he said mournfully.

'We're not done yet,' I said brightly, 'It might mean Plan A is off, but there's always Plan B, isn't there?'

'What is Plan B, exactly?' asked Tariq.

Genghis put down his gun and lit a cigarette. 'I'll come back to you on that one,' he growled, puffing smoke rings.

Tariq began freewheeling wildly. 'What we need is some

influence, the backing of someone powerful, someone on our side, a great man, and one with impeccable contacts.'

'That's what I was going to say,' piped up the old man grudgingly.

'I know just the man,' said Genghis, more animatedly than I had ever heard him speaking. 'I don't know why I didn't think of him before.'

Ahmed, meanwhile, was looking even more irritated. 'Who is it exactly?' he said, trying not to look interested.

A round of wild guessing ensued.

'Dostum,' roared Genghis at last.

'Dostum!' cried the others in dismay.

'Dostum?' I said weakly. 'Who's he?'

'He's a warlord,' said Tariq, apart from that remaining tight-lipped on the subject.

'The General, of course, knows everyone. If anyone can help us, it is him,' added Genghis.

Another bout of questioning began, this time less inhibited, the men increasingly heated, before a series of loud, animated exchanges, knowing glances and sudden whisperings.

'So what are the risks?' I asked, finally managing to get a word in edgeways.

'The usual – the mines, the bombs, the hijack, the insects, the lack of facilities, the languages, the heat,' they all chimed.

'Nothing out of the ordinary, then,' I said matter-of-factly.

'No,' said everyone simultaneously.

'But the Taliban have a much weaker footing in the north. Surely it's safer there?'

'Slightly.' sighed Tariq, 'We will need bribes. We will

need intermediaries. Above all, we will need Allah!' he said, motioning upwards with his forefinger. 'You will have to wear a burka again, for all our sakes.'

'It went well last time . . .'

'Even then . . .'

'And even then, what?'

'You are a defenceless little thing,' agreed Genghis.

'You mean I am a woman?' I said, fixing him with a piercing look.

'There will be places you are not allowed to go.'

'We can go round them . . .'

'There are no – er – toilet facilities,' said Genghis finally.

'I see,' I said, and left it there.

★ ☽ ★

Two days later we were standing on the runway of Kabul airport. It was just the three of us: myself, Genghis and Tariq. The silent nephews were staying behind in Kabul.

It was less of a plane than a plastic Airfix model, stuck together at the seams and half-painted. Nevertheless, all seats were taken. There were turbans and veils, and the odd *pakol* hat, one of which belonged to Tariq. The men slipped on their Raybans, and more and more sunglasses began popping up around us.

We lifted off into an opalescent sky. Beneath us white peaks lay in dollops as if fashioned by giant ice-cream scoops. Dotted around them forgotten settlements nestling in deserted valleys made sprinkles. I chewed on a date, worrying about Maryam, wondering if the trip would be worth it, or if we were already too late.

We were not long into the flight when the plane began shaking. Another hefty bout of lurching, and agitated conversations were starting up among people who had never met before and who had been trying not to begin them in the first place. Tariq began clutching the arms of his seat with whitened knuckles, trying not to look out of the window – or, for that matter, at Genghis, who looked equally ashen, eyes screwed, whiskers a-quiver as, from time to time, the plane reeled and lurched.

A tense hour ensued as the engine chugged noisily, interspersed with worrying periods when nothing could be heard at all. At last, on the approach to Mazar-e-Sharif, the co-pilot suddenly got out of his seat and steadied himself, clearing his throat and addressing us. The crosswinds were surprisingly strong for this time of year, he said gravely, visibility was poor owing to some unexpected low-lying cloud, and because of a technical hitch some of the communications equipment was not working. But they would give it their best. From then on, conversations dwindled somewhat.

The plane began its descent into fog. Genghis's brown face turned green while Tariq began muttering the *Fatiha*. The wings tilted to the right and then to the left and then levelled. The mist cleared and we felt a bump, and then another one. Audible sighs and relieved chatterings rippled round as we taxied slowly to the control tower, but it was a while before I realised I was the only one clapping.

★ ☽ ★

Mazar seemed an archaic city, reminiscent of the capital, but more peaceful. Pony traps jangled, mopeds chuffed, bicycles tinkled. The scent of spices mingled with fumes, sewage, and freshly baked *naan*, with its smell of life and taste of heaven. Faces seemed more subdued here, but there were fewer soldiers. Venerable old men strode past wearing turbans and *chapans*, long striped gowns, their sandals curling at the end like a moth's proboscis. Where once they had sported daggers and swords at their sides, today they sported mobile telephones. Giant posters of Dostum hung from windows and rooftops, his gaze meeting ours with Orwellian intimidation. I wondered what he would be like.

Tariq took the wheel of the hired Datsun jeep, while Genghis divested himself of the light machine-gun he had smuggled on to the plane with a cluster of dollars. He slung it in the boot defiantly, climbed in and stuck his feet out of the window as we drove.

Beyond the town lay an isolated culture. A tattered sign read '*Afghanistan Qabrestan-e Amreekaiha*', Afghanistan is the graveyard of the Americans. I shivered as I translated the words, overwhelmed by an unexpected grief. I had seen terrible poverty in Kabul, but this was heartbreaking.

The wheels clattered on. Around us the landscape stretched emptily, existing as if in the shade of everything that was missing, the shade cast by war. The wind was soundless, but it felt as if the silence was temporary and untrusted. Long periods passed when the signal for my mobile faded, until it disappeared altogether. Mile upon mile of villages lay shattered, uninhabitable because of the many mines still unexploded. Men squatted, motionless, gazing into the distance. One prayed by the roadside, facing Mecca, while behind him a bird pecked at the ground as if in imitation.

It was stifling. Sometimes I peeled off the burka and wrapped my scarf about my face. It would have to do for now, or I'd flake out from heat exhaustion. The men didn't seem to notice the temperature, laughing and joking, practising their English.

The road stretched endlessly, as if into nothingness, as if it might reach to the end of the world. Parched, barren land gave way to a steppe ablaze with crops and flowers. Far-off children in bright clothing stood out like tiny anemones. A loose collection of buildings rose from the horizon, shafts of ochre emerging, phoenix-like, from the haze. Shiberghan was an unassuming town, but it had roots in ancient Bactria, where the Greeks had waged war, and later the Kushans. Treasure had been discovered here – the famous Bactrian Gold, a trove to rival that of the Pharaohs. The locals were proud of something arguably more precious: melons. Marco Polo once wrote that they were the best and the most plentiful.

At the rundown checkpoint our smiles met with blank expressions. It was useless trying to charm them. Phrases word-perfect in Dari inside my head, 'I agree with everything you say' and 'Thank you for showing me your wonderful gun', were destined to remain there. It was up to Genghis to utter the magic words. 'We are here to pay court to the great warlord, General Abdul Rashid Dostum, head of the Uzbek tribe,' he beamed, and the soldiers ushered us through.

Chapter 15

'Because of the Friend his Dog is Welcomed'

از روی دوست سگش نیکوست

A knock at the heavily guarded gates, a clattering of footsteps, then nothing. My heart began beating again. Another set of footsteps, this time nearer, and it stopped again, before eventually the soldiers emerged. The guns were slung down, and the shouting began, then loud snorts of laughter. Genghis was being welcomed like a long-lost brother. He had come to visit his old friends, the General's bodyguards. They had been brothers in the war with the Soviets.

'*Yak teer-o do fakhta*,' whispered Tariq. It was an old Afghan saying that meant 'One arrow, two finches'. I just hoped there wasn't any killing involved.

After a shyly administered body frisk, from which I was mercifully excluded, we were led up a steep stone staircase. At the top lay a central courtyard. There were fountains, pools and a building made entirely of glass with elaborate columns and mirrors. A dark-haired man, thickset and with a bushy moustache, was holding court beside a swimming pool befitting a Hollywood mansion. Word had it that General Dostum had a laugh like a thunder-roll, a surprising penchant for a glass of whisky, and a past as formidable as it was murky, but as he greeted us warmly he seemed quite charming.

'Today you are honorary man,' he smiled, after the men had exchanged courtesies. 'You must stay and have dinner.'

'Thank you,' I said, receiving the invitation uncertainly, only later learning from Tariq that it meant I had special dispensation to mix and speak freely with the men.

★ ☽ ★

Dinner was a grand affair. Servant boys bore trays piled high with delicacies. Venison, camel and mutton were washed down with vodka, whisky and tea that tasted of the firewood used to heat it. Ordinary Afghans lived on rice, although many didn't have enough of it, but here the *palau* glistened, jewel-like, with amber carrot, silvered almonds and emerald pistachios. The bread was round and glazed, the dough etched with patterns, and there were sweets and dried fruit.

High above the struggles of the poor, Dostum's circle shimmered in luxury. There were raconteurs, a vodka expert, and a magician to amuse the guests who were largely men, except for the occasional and relatively silent wife. Guests were ordered in rank the correct distance from the General, who sat furthest from the door in the place of honour, dressed in a robe and an army jacket.

Nearby sat the richest man in Asia whose name I didn't catch, and the ambassadors of Russia, and Uzbekistan. To my left sat an elderly man, a Mullah and an *akhund*, a religious leader, dressed all in white apart from yellow socks that gave prominence to his tiny feet in contrast to his over-sized turban. The socks were supposed to be skin-coloured, he confessed in almost perfect English, but his skin was yellow, so he'd bought yellow ones instead.

'You should not be here alone,' he said worriedly. 'Women are not as strong as men.'

'Are you saying men are better than them?'

'According to the Qur'an, men have only a degree of advantage over them. It's not that much.'

I frowned at him hard.

'Women are the same everywhere,' interrupted Dostum, who had overheard us and was laughing. 'They all empty our pockets!'

'My pockets have eyes!' replied the Mullah, flashing a yellow molar.

'Yes, but we all know they're blind!' thundered Dostum, and as silence fell soft on his audience it was only now that I saw why he was known so widely as the Lion of Mazar.

The men placed sticky Afghan tobacco into pieces of paper, rolled them and twisted them at the end, while Dostum held court for a while. The foreign forces were hypocritical, claiming to uphold freedom and justice, but they had come with their own agendas of power and control. The occupation was not really about stopping the extremists; it was much more complicated and far-reaching, just like it had been for their brothers in Iraq. If the Americans could control Afghanistan, they could control the rest of the Muslim world, and that was what they wanted.

We listened attentively and, I, for one, silently. If I had commented on the war I would be making ill-informed judgements on things I didn't exactly understand in front of strange people who spoke different languages.

The debate in full sway, I slunk off unnoticed . . . A sudden scurrying of footsteps behind, and I jumped round on tenterhooks. Behind me the Mullah was chattering excitedly, rattling off his sentences like speeding railway carriages. All of his children had inherited his intellect, his determination, his good looks. He did not like, he loved: the sky, the Americans, himself. His eyes rolled, yellow semi-circles of agitation, and then he breathed heavily, as a peculiar hubris formed the climax of his soliloquy. As an infidel, my damned soul would go to hell, he warned. If I married him now it would be saved. He would make a good husband. He was rich: he had two hundred sheep, six hundred goats, sixty camels and two rocket-launchers. Above all, he was grateful.

I smiled weakly, as he finally allowed me to speak. 'It is a most kind and generous offer . . .' I said ruefully.

'Thank you,' he said nonchalantly, without waiting for me to finish. He had considered it very carefully and the more he thought it over, the more convinced he had become that his judgement was the correct one.

'. . . but an infidel wife would be an independent one.'

His eyes grew wild in disbelief. His pockets hadn't seen that one coming.

★ ☽ ★

A bevy of guards had materialised from nowhere. I couldn't help wondering if they were the same ones that Tariq said had raped the women of Kabul in 1991. Their expressions were deadpan, as they frogmarched me to my quarters. I bade them goodnight and they nodded politely.

The room was decorated in ormolu and red. A portrait of Karzai stared down intently, seeming to wink in the decaying light. As I slipped into bed my father's voice was in my head again. I remembered a letter he had sent me when I was a child. I had been away at school and afraid of the dark. 'Catch the breeze in the flickering of a candle,' he had written. 'In the darkness always remember the safe light is there for you any time you need it.'

I knew now that he was right, for however frightening the darkness might seem, there was always a light, even if it was hiding – bright, comforting and safe. The safe light was love. That love seemed very far off now, but in the dark, grey light it was like a beacon.

A crow landed at the window, squawked, and flew off. Finally I fell into an uneasy slumber, waking several hours later to a burst of distant gunfire. I was glad to see the light of daybreak.

★ ☽ ★

Qala-e Jangi lay a few miles west of Mazar. It was General Dostum's military headquarters. Only now did the stories begin to emerge, the ones that made my hair stand on end, my stomach turn and my heart thump. Only now did they mention that it was at Dostum's command that women had been raped, mutilated, and killed during the devastation of Kabul in 1994; that it was at the place we were going that two thousand Taliban prisoners had been asphyxiated when Dostum's troops packed them into shipping containers just a few years earlier. Only now did they recount how Taliban prisoners had been captured, tortured and murdered by the Northern Alliance, and that those atrocities had taken place where we were heading. One was known as 'dead men dancing' they said: victims were beheaded, petrol was poured down their necks and set alight as blood spurted out and the bodies jerked in their death throes. Skinning alive was another favourite. Then there were the cannons fired from the fort with prisoners tied to the muzzles, they said, peering at my face as it twisted in horror. As the sloping mud ramparts of the fort loomed, it was clear this was no fairy tale.

Inside the high walls elders, religious scholars and holy men from different tribes gathered, their faces worn like their second-hand shoes, gestured with hands and smiles in dialects I didn't quite grasp about relationships I couldn't exactly understand. Some of them had walked miles to be here, but I sensed the place in which they felt most at home was the past.

A guest was causing a commotion. With his long, white gown and rough, bushy beard, he reminded me of Tolkien's Gandalf. Tired faces brightened as he approached the assembly. I wondered if it had something to do with the glittery slippers he had just slipped off, or the multi-coloured dyed toenails now resplendently laid bare. Tariq knew him immediately. He was Abdul Saleem, a well-known former Taliban commander and Mujahedin guerrilla, a veteran of bitter tribal feuds and bloody battle. He had been nicknamed 'Rocketi' on account of his passion for firing Stinger missiles against the Russians. His relationship with the Taliban had ended when he had swapped sides. Now he was Governor of Musa Qala. Like

Dostum, he was everyone's friend.

Saleem sprinkled verses from the Qur'an into his thoughts and his statements. The elders were anxious. Their country no longer belonged to them, they said gravely. Clucking his tongue and pontificating, he wooed the elders and scholars with a bouquet of promises. As he was whisked off in a flurry of bows, dust, turbans and Kalashnikov rifles, I worried how he would possibly be able to keep them.

We had been told by Dostum's advisers to be brief, and when our turn came, Dostum received us formally. With a flash of his epaulettes, he signalled one of his servants to fetch some tea. Genghis and Tariq talked business and Dostum's eyes flickered as if he knew something. He came straight to the point, picking his words with considered precision. Such matters were tribal, he said gravely. There were rules and relationships. The tribes had their own justice.

Genghis smiled wryly. When it came to justice, General Dostum had his own way of dealing with things. He had once punished a soldier for stealing by tying the man to the tracks of a Russian tank that drove around the courtyard crushing his body to a pulp, while Dostum watched.

'Are you able to help us, then?' asked Tariq, passing his hand about his *karakul* hat.

Dostum nodded, but it was at Genghis that he directed his answer. 'Enquiries shall be made. You have my word. We shall come back to you.' The men bowed their courtesies and we made our retreat. 'Stay away from the southern compound,' he called out after us. 'Taliban fighters might still be alive there. They are suicidal people and you should expect anything of them.'

A soldier told us to move on. While we were reluctant to

leave empty-handed, there seemed little point in waiting. With Genghis poised for a phone call, we decided to head back to Kabul. Genghis had goodbyes to say, so we arranged to meet him at the gate. We made our way out, flanked by Dostum's armed fighters. As we wound our way slowly through the passages and stairwells I began to worry. Something didn't feel right. I was aware of moving downwards, of our footsteps echoing. On the well-trodden ground I saw a torn, damp rag, and a stain of what looked like blood.

What were the soldiers saying? There was no time for translation, nor even for Tariq's secret-weapon smile. Shouts echoed like the lost voices of men who had died there. As we turned to go the other way, one of them blocked our path with his rifle. My mind went blank. I was aware only of the beads of sweat prickling on the back of my neck and across the top of my back. A distant clatter of footsteps grew louder. Another soldier, tall, bearded, approached and began speaking. 'There has been a misunderstanding,' he said apologetically. The guards stood back, Genghis appeared, and then everyone breathed again.

I ran up to the ramparts and tore back my scarf. Across the plain a sandstorm was brewing, but the wind was still, and the sounds that reached us were distant. Genghis twitched his moustache and sighed.

'What did you say to them?' seemed a not unreasonable question in the circumstances.

'I told them not to treat my wife like that,' he said.

'That was very presumptuous of you,' I said, realising he meant me, but as I looked sideways at his kind, dark eyes, it was impossible to be cross with him.

CHAPTER 16

'Little Drops Make the River'

قطره قطره دریا میشود

It was raining in Kabul. The land the colour of yellow emery board, green tanks and Rothko red carpets had become a canvas of browns. A few birds were splashing in the dirty pools that had formed. Others tried to clean their wings in the rivulets of mud that washed the streets. Outside the hotel a woman squatted, her burka drenched, but as a four-wheel drive roared past, the only thing her arms received was a spattering of mud. I turned out my pockets, helpless to wash away her problems.

A week of ennui set in. We waited restlessly, with a feeling of unease between the emptiness of the past and the shrinking expanse of the future, all the while conscious of the decreasing avenues we feared would stay unexplored forever. General Dostum remained silent, and the men were praying harder for answers that continued to evade them. It was Allah's will, they said, though no one knew what that meant. None of us had any idea who held Zaki, where he was being held, or whether he was alive or dead. For Sohaila it was a disaster: there was still technically an engagement, but as things stood the wedding looked as if it were off. Should she look for another suitor? Should they wait? Maryam was bearing up bravely, stirring her tea with her spoon so that it tinkled sweetly as if trying to cheer us all up, but if you looked carefully into her eyes you could see the tension.

With the days passing and our options diminishing, I sensed I had promised more than I could deliver. I thought long and hard about whether to leave, but in the end something prevented me. I lay awake listening to the rain, and my thoughts ran like the raindrops that trickled down the wall of my room. I stayed still like a pool, no feeling beyond the watery sounds, until they became small, like beads of water on the brim of my sleep – my family, my father's health, and the dog that I had seen at the zoo. I walked, squelching past sodden sandbags, and my shoes in the mud, like everything else that was stuck. I tried to take solace in the words of Anton Chekhov who once wrote: 'Take life pace by pace, slowly, slowly, and leave the competition to others,' though I knew underneath it was impossible, because I was competing with myself.

★ ☽ ★

The sun came up and the air cleared, freshened by snowy peaks. High above the city, life felt better. We tried hard to distract ourselves, treading the ground of a well-worn path. The path snaked from the towers of a fort. You could see for miles. The geography of the city was laid bare, the land undulating from the airport in the north to the NATO bases to the east, the war-torn provinces of the south, and slums blending with the sandy ridge below.

Tariq walked bravely ahead, dodging what looked like spent ammunition lying on the ground, his sister and I carefully placing our tread in his footsteps. Bala Hissar was an ancient fort, he said, where the Taliban had held their arsenal, where the Mujahedin had captured weapons from the Soviets. The British had once held it in Victoria's forgotten wars.

Maryam gazed wistfully into the distance as she spoke. 'I've something to show you,' she said. We made our way down, through streets filled with the stench of rubbish, where open sewers poured along gutters. Only the odd crimson of a kite flashing in the sky, or a bright garment on a clothing line relieved the monotony of beige.

And then, suddenly we saw it.

The garden lay beyond high mud walls, a sanctuary within them. Hirsute men in striped gowns sat on benches. A horde of infants dashed around: a gardener prayed in the flowerbeds; birds chirruped about the trees; mottled yellow butterflies flew as if puzzled to find themselves in such a wondrous place as this. Buds and petals seemed to dance in raised beds of jasmine and pomegranate, of sweet-smelling herbs, dwarf irises, and flowers with petals like candy floss. The garden was laid out in a classical *charbagh* (four-garden) pattern. Long avenues of plane, cypress and poplar trees outlined gravel paths, their straight and measured lines reflecting the order of the universe. Everything was held in balance, defined and sheltered.

These were Babur's Gardens, said Tariq, as if he owned them. After the war with the Soviets nothing had remained except an empty field of shell holes and the odd tree stump; but the garden had been restored. In a city of such hardship, this place of beauty felt all the more hard-won. Genghis expressed it differently. There was an old Afghan song he growled. He fiddled with his turban, cleared his throat and honked. 'The camel needed its dates and the earth its flowers . . .'

As Genghis began in his out-of-tune basso, Tariq ran off. We strained to keep up with his nimble footsteps and soon he was a just a blip against the graduated line of a white marble watercourse. As we finally reached the top, he popped up again. 'This is the Emperor Babur's tomb,' he announced, not in the least out of breath. His interest was grabbed by a small marble screen. 'His last wish was to lie serenaded by birdsong, his tomb uncovered so that the rain and sun could beat upon it.' Babur's wishes had been ignored, it seemed, for the tomb had been buried by generations of his family under a pavilion, later almost destroyed by the war. Now restored, those wishes had finally been fulfilled. Maryam read the inscription out loud: 'Built for the light garden of the angel king who was forgiven by God and whose rest is in the garden of paradise.' It cheered us all and it even stopped Genghis singing.

Tariq had leapt ahead again, running fast like a sprightly young mountain goat. Only Pashtun had voices like nightingales, he cooed. Uzbeks and Tajiks sang like cats. He was craning his neck and bending down to squint at something, a sign, the writing faded by the beating sun. As he read it out loud he had to say it twice in his own language before I would believe it, and it was only on the third rendition that, seeing the confused expression upon my face, it popped out in English. *Love's Labour's Lost* was to be performed in Dari. It was the first time that

Shakespeare had been put on in Afghanistan since the Soviet invasion of 1978.

I jumped up and down, cheering like a maniac. 'We must go!' I cried excitedly. Tariq frowned uncertainly, smoothing the sprouts of his aspiring moustache and wrinkling his nose. His uncle didn't approve of the theatre. It spoke to him of witching arts and evil things. Plays, especially those with music, and, God forbid, dancing, led good men and women astray, took their mind off devotional life and removed their thoughts from God. 'What was this Mister who wrote plays like, anyway?' he said half-heartedly. Was he a real sheikh?

'Well,' said I said, 'he wasn't exactly a sheikh. Actually he was a bit like Babur, equally fond of young boys, but he could write better.' Tariq seemed satisfied with the answer, so I left it there.

★ ☽ ★

It was a few more days before we finally decided to give it a whirl. The evening was cool, the garden enchanted. The sun hung low in the sky, and peeked through openings among the branches of the trees, defined and clear. A scent freshened the griminess of the air. I wondered if it might be rosemary.

It was just the three of us – Maryam, Tariq and myself. Genghis, being a traditional sort of chap, had passed. He had business to attend to, and, having delegated responsibility for his sheep to his nephews, was going to check on them. By that he meant the nephews rather than the sheep. Sohaila and Ahmed were also not coming, having

129

decided it was best to abstain.

The audience was a motley assortment of grand-looking people of various tribal descents, foreign-looking people, and shifty types sporting rifles like umbrellas. They were gossiping feverishly, loudly lamenting the risks and the dangers. Actresses here were in fear of their lives. One had been forced to leave home, thought to be guilty of adultery or prostitution because she was returning late after the long rehearsals. It was a different world from the pretences of Hollywood.

We made our way to our various seating areas, Tariq with the men in the best seats and Maryam and myself with the women in the back rows, as a hushed excitement descended. Oval faces with delicate features flickered on stage, shyly avoiding each other's gaze. The actors delivered their lines with stately grace. Words and phrases beyond me in Shakespeare's English took on a surreal quality in their foreign renderings, as if carrying more meaning through their expression in a strange language. Pauses echoed like the titters of those listening who strained to grasp them. The script had been edited. The Russians had become Indians. Lines such as 'Madame, you are a goddess,' had mysteriously vanished, characters tempered to become more acceptable.

As the play reached its climax the actors relaxed slightly. Wooden gestures became fluid. Speeches were uttered with feeling, and the resounding finale dazzled with Bollywood dance routines. Across in the shadows an owl hooted, a bad omen in these parts.

I glanced over at Tariq and he smiled back uncertainly. The play was amusing, he said later, although it wasn't meant to be. Shakespeare was not bad, but there could never be a drama like the theatre of life.

★ ☽ ★

'I'd like to come,' said Sohaila bravely, glancing ahead as if gazing towards a distant country only she herself had visited. I guessed that place was the old days, when families went to films together, and even had their own boxes, a place before the Taliban came to power.

We were on a roll. Tariq and Maryam had suggested it. Naturally I myself had been up for it, and finally Ahmed gave in to it. 'As long as you put on your burkas,' he cautioned, as he reluctantly gave his permission for the trip. We all nodded sheepishly. 'We don't want any trouble,' we said. Later that week we slunk off like truant teenagers, while the little ones stayed at home. It would be unwise to expose the children to such risky influences.

The Ariana Cinema had been abandoned for years because the Taliban outlawed its activities. Cinemas were places of ill repute. Word had it that the staff had fought back, hiding the original tapes in the ceilings, squirreling away the best ones, at great risk to themselves and their families, in the labyrinth of basement rooms, and telling the police that the cassettes had been stolen. Today it prided itself on being Afghanistan's most modern cinema. There had already been a Russian week, and Japanese and German weeks, but there were no plans for an Afghan week. That would be a step too far.

What looked like a black-and-white photo of Massoud loomed between rogues from martial arts and war films. A bikini-clad heroine, bottom half over-pinned with a piece of paper for modesty, gazed seductively from the wall among the real women concealed in burkas. Squashed in between the Bollywood epics was a somewhat more familiar poster. *Titanic* had a dedicated following in Kabul, and a poster of Kate Winslet had been tastefully adapted with felt-tip pens to make it acceptable for the Afghan market, all cleavage obliterated. At the bottom someone had written, 'Romance beyond all Imagines' in wobbly English letters. Sadly, we had missed it. Instead we were to be treated to *A Star is Born*. No doubt it was especially for the foreign-aid workers, sighed Tariq. Was Judy Garland a Muslim?

At the counter a turbaned man offered tea from a huge metal teapot. Beside him men, similarly turbaned, chatted furiously, shaking their heads and scratching their beards in their usual routines. As we made our way to our separate seating areas a limping guard frisked the men for weapons, but not the women. What if we were hiding Kalashnikovs under our burkas? No one would have found them.

After a flipping of seats and a tangible buzz, the tape flickered, and the sound system emitted a high-pitched scream. As we lifted up our visors, the women ducked shyly away from the projection beam as it flashed about the auditorium. The screen descended into a murky fuzz while the occasional blurry shadow flitted and jarred. At last the picture settled. Mesmerised by the dancing, Maryam's wide-eyed face grew pale against the shadows. Her mother seemed equally transfixed, but in no time at all her head tilted slightly. The plastic bag at her side emblazoned with the words 'Super Fashionable You' slid gradually to the floor, accompanied by the soft snuffles of snoring. It was only at the end, when the music became loud that she woke with a jolt and began applauding.

Afterwards, Tariq was luke warm about the movie. Men preferred war films, the ones that taught them the skills of battle, how to plan an attack, how to evade the enemy. The women thought differently. For them, it was neither war nor films that taught them the rules of living. It was marriage.

CHAPTER 17

'When Man is Perplexed, God is Benevolent'

هیچ کاری خالی از خیر نیست

Genghis needed a cigarette to clear his lungs. He lit up and began puffing. Meanwhile, Tariq was fumbling with the cornucopia of phones in his pocket, finally finding the one that was ringing. He switched on the hands-free, but I still didn't catch a word of it. Afterwards he explained. The caller had been one of Dostum's men. A hostage was being held outside Herat, said the man. He believed it was Zaki, and that he was alive and in good health. We should make no mistake: the threat to his life was real. Any involvement from the authorities, direct or otherwise, would result in the immediate cessation of good will, and increase the likelihood of Taliban involvement. At the same time, we ourselves were free to go and look for Zaki if we wanted to. They could guarantee our safety as far as Faryab, but after that we were on our own.

The men punched the air and Sohaila began cheering, while I myself sat haloed in a Ready brek glow. Only one face in the room remained uncertain, head shaking cautiously, hands clasped as if in resistance. Seeing his sister's reaction, Tariq bent down close to her, his voice suddenly gentle. It would be all right, he said. Allah would never desert us. He was just testing us.

With the end to inertia and anxiety came a warm shower of optimism, which inevitably meant time for another pot of tea. As Sohaila poured, Tariq began pacing, rattling off a plan with the precision of a military commander. Travel via the Kandahar-Herat highway would be suicidal. A four-by-four could go most places, but it was no journey for a woman. A female journalist had been attacked by masked men and had her arms lacerated. Herat was crawling with Taliban, and the danger could not be underestimated. So Genghis and I would go by plane, while Tariq would stay behind to speak to the officials, then catch up with us later.

We were to stay with a friend. There was an old tutor of his in Herat, a Sufi, a philosopher and a scientist, with an intellect that was as broad as he was tall. He had constructed an astrolabe, calculated the latitude of his village, and in his spare time taught the art of mathematics and philosophy according to Galen and Aristotle. Ismael was a good man who would be sure to help us. Maryam would stay behind, of course. Also obvious was the decision to omit Genghis's nephews. It wasn't that they didn't need them, said the men. They had sheep to attend to.

★ ☽ ★

Tariq dropped me off in the old quarter and I made my way through the maze of streets. Enticed by the scent of *khaste shireen*, almonds sweetened with caramel, and *noqul*, sugar-coated nuts, I ventured into the pastry shop, emerging later with arms laden, into the searing light where a cluster of children soon relieved me of my burden. Empty-handed, I turned left, glanced into the shadows, and halted.

A tilt of the head, a doleful wag of the tail, and my heart leapt. It couldn't be, could it? The ears pricked, the legs contracted, and the dog stood upright. It was her. Cocking her head, she let out a whimper and rolled on her back. I reached into my bag and took out some bread, crumbled it and put it down. The dog sniffed deeply. I bent forward and stretched out my hand to allow her to sniff me. She hesitated, retreated a little, and though she opened her mouth, nothing came but a silent bark. I stepped back, and the dog stepped forward. I stepped forward again, very gently this time as the dog stepped back again. So it went on, this strange, nervous dancing, until I walked to the corner of the street where a charcoal-burner was sizzling, and bought a *boulanee*, pastry stuffed with vegetables and leeks, and placed it down. There. At last she was eating.

Turbaned men were watching, stopping, pointing. What was I doing feeding a dog when there were people starving, they muttered. Had I gone crazy? What about the children? Why didn't I feed them instead? As I slipped away, I had nothing to say to them. They were right, of course.

★ ☽ ★

I was still upset when we boarded the Herat flight. The plane glided effortlessly, as behind us Kabul faded into the distance. Head in a book that I was pretending to read, my head was in a whirl. I felt ashamed of myself, my weakness, my inability to do anything good in the world. I felt I had failed the dog, like I had failed the man who had died in the square the day of the bus bombing. Now I was probably failing Maryam and Zaki, too. I couldn't save any of them.

At last we were turning to land, the city beneath us gleaming at the heart of a wide open plain, around it some of the wildest-looking and most magnificent scenery I had ever seen. To the north were the mountains and the steppes; to the east peaks equally daunting were splintered with the silvery tendrils of a river; to the south and west the desert lands stretched out into infinity. Genghis wasn't looking. He had turned olive to match his olive shirt. We seemed to ascend and then dive again. We churned and juddered and, as I said my prayers, finally came down safely.

Herat airport seemed more like a large shed. Outside was the familiar littering of old fighter planes and war scrap, bullet-scarred and ruined mud cubes with their high slit windows and straw roofs. Remnants of mosques dotted the skyline. Derelict buildings wearily stood to attention at the roadside as if they didn't know what they were supposed to be doing there. Herodotus had called this city the bread-basket of central Asia, but from the air it had seemed more like a laundry basket, full of crumpled clothes in need of ironing.

The venerable old gentleman who met us was Tariq's friend the Sufi, his hollow face framed by a perfectly manicured beard. Beneath it he wore a *chapan,* a long striped robe of turquoise silk. He smiled courteously, placing his right hand on his heart as I returned the greeting, but forgetting my manners I accidentally looked at him. He turned his head sideways.

'I'm sorry,' I said, 'I hope I have not offended you . . .'

'Not at all,' he said quickly, wiping his eye as if something was suddenly caught in it. 'It was your use of the subjunctive that touched me.'

I warmed to him immediately. It was only what I had been taught to say. The exact phrase, *omid waram shoma ra narahat nakardah baasham*, contained an element of doubt, and this was reflected in the subjunctive mood, which had almost completely fallen out of everyday usage, as it had done in many languages. I loved that he appreciated it.

Ismael's Lada moaned like Tariq's sidecar, along to Genghis's snoring and the tinkling bells of horse-drawn carriages straight out of *Doctor Zhivago*. Traffic lights were working, though everyone was ignoring them, and the roads seemed less rutted than in Kabul. As the city fell behind us, the scenery, at first arid, grew more fertile. In the distance vineyards and melon beds, orchards and wheat fields, made up a patchwork of browns and purples, a vista of rounded slopes where mud and boulders had fallen in the sweep of the winter avalanches. Beyond them lay cliffs sprinkled with gnarled pistachio trees, carved by the wind into unlikely leanings. Further away still lay the lofty peaks, guarding it all.

Ismael whiled away the journey by trying out his English on me, his arms swirling as I imagined they might in one of his devotional dances. It turned out that he had been a great friend of Massoud, with whom he had fought in the Panjshir valley. His order, the Qadirriyah, looked after a holy site, the shrine of Guzar Gah. If there was time, he would take us there. People walked miles to it, the sick and the dying, the crippled, the despairing, he said, but the real disease they suffered from was incurable. It was the disease of war.

The village of Karukh lay invisible from the road, sheltered by tall pines, with a scattering of bullet-studded mud buildings nestling beneath the ridges. A goatherd drove his scrawny animals along the track, in front a king goat, shaggy and majestic with his great horns. Behind trotted a large dog, a mastiff, rounding them up. I shouted in Genghis's ear and he opened his eyes blearily. 'How many times have I told you not to call me that!' he roared crossly. He didn't mean it, he then added, grinning.

We made our way on foot along a tiny mountain pathway beside a rivulet filled with fresh watercress. Mulberry trees stood alongside junipers in a ring of protection around the compound. Coils of barbed wire entangled themselves with the roses and geraniums. The house itself hid in the shade of a *chenar* tree, its crooked walls embedded in the rock as if growing out of it. Ismael himself slept in one half, while the other was shelter for his donkey, two goats and his generous brood of chickens. Inside, the chamber was bare except for an old chandelier whose branches dropped like icicles from a solitary light bulb.

We sat cross-legged on a patchwork of donkey bags as Ismael told his story. He lived alone and in hiding because of his beliefs; he was still in fear of the Taliban, many of his brothers having been beaten savagely and thrown into prison. The Sufis had been central in the religious life of Afghanistan for many centuries, but in the eyes of the Taliban they were still infidels. He was at a loss to know why. When it came to religion there was no question but that Allah loved everyone, young and old, good and bad, Muslim and Sufi. Even Christians.

As Ismael spoke of his losses, his eyes filled with sadness, lifting only slightly when I handed him a tin of tea from Fortnum & Mason and a jar of comb honey. But it was the packets of Marlboro Lights that widened them sufficiently to reveal their bloodshot whites. He searched around for something to give me in return, his eyes fluttering across the room to a shelf of little treasures in the corner – a tiny painting, brightly coloured in a gilt frame, a strange wooden pipe, a highwayman's pistol. Then his hand alighted on something, a book small enough to fit in a pocket, its feathery worn pages illuminated in gold and jewel-like colours, and barely held together by ancient leather covers finished with stamped decorations. The Kufic lettering was twisted, floriated, knotted, intertwined. Normally, he confessed, he kept it hidden in his donkey's nosebag, but he knew I was coming so he'd dug it out specially. He knew it would be good for me. There was no truer love than the contemplation of beauty, he said; it was a gift bestowed by Allah himself.

The book was beautiful because it was sacred. It was the Holy Qu'ran, after all. He peered at a page pensively. The words were what mattered. The best scribes would devote years to copying the sacred text. The early calligraphers had searched for styles of writing that would be worthy of the Qur'an's content, and the same applied to the inks. They used fine pigments – lapis for blue, indigo for dark blue, azurite for light blue, malachite and verdigris (made by dipping copper plates in vinegar and burying them) for greens. Mercury and sulphur or ground cinnabar were used for vermilion. Yellow was made from orpiment, and red lead plus carbon boiled with gall nuts gave the black ink. Some pigments were not stable: silver would tarnish and go black; lead and azurite dissolved the paper. The brushwork was so fine because the brushes used were made of hair from a squirrel's tail, or, finest of all from a Persian cat, threaded through a quill. He had tried it once with the hairs of his own cat, but it hadn't worked, and the cat hadn't thought much of it either.

I gazed at the book admiringly. I had always been taught that Islamic art was about learning and skill rather than divine inspiration, the reverse of Plato's view of the artist as the recipient of a vision or metaphysical idea from God. The artist was a simply a spokesperson expressing the vision of God. The artist's mission was inextricable from the Qur'an.

Ismael nodded sagely. 'Take it,' he said, handing it to me.

I looked at him disbelievingly. 'Thank you, but I couldn't possibly . . .'

'Please, it is my honour,' he insisted.

'Thank you again,' I said, passing it back, 'but I just cannot.'

'I'll have it!' piped up Genghis expectantly,

'Why are you afraid to take it?' asked Ismael, ignoring him.

'It is too precious.'

'It is unwise to be too attached – to things, or to people.'

I knew he was right. Even so I handed the book back to him. Suddenly I felt desperately homesick, and as he piled sugar into our tea there was nothing to sweeten the feeling.

Over supper of fruit soup, a traditional dish in these parts, we spoke of religion, the men puffing smooth rings of tobacco, Ismael summing up the differences of Islam with the insight of a master. I had to admire him. I had always imagined that a great mind combined knowledge with creativity and imagination, but, for Ismael, true intelligence was able to exploit both in the name of religion. If Islam was the dogmatic father, he said calmly, I was to think of Sufism as a kind-hearted godfather. Whereas Islamic law provided a social structure, Sufism was concerned with the inner path. Its followers took the Qur'an and the traditions, and enriched them with mystical meaning. There were other differences, too. Whereas Islam was submission to the Divine Law, Sufism was about surrender. Islam talked of sin, Sufism spoke of heedlessness. A holy warrior prepared himself for life after death, a Sufi master strove for a spiritual death in this life. It was to be a life of devotion and prayer, forsaking the world in the name of belief.

As Ismael pronounced, Genghis looked non-plussed. Allah was great, he said, and that was all you needed to know.

The breeze became cold, and the slow hum of cicadas echoed in the shrubbery. A few lights appeared at the base of the valley, blurring slightly, moving, twisting, twinkling in the fading light like fireflies. We watched them as they grew larger. As the sound of boots and men's voices came closer outside on the pathway, suddenly it became clear. The figure stepped forward, and when the shadow lifted, I could have sworn it was someone I knew, the turn of the head, the gait ... It couldn't be my father. Then, as I looked again, I saw it was Tariq.

CHAPTER 18

'Don't Take off Your Shoes Without Investigating the Water'

آب را نادیده حوزه را از با نکش

We set off in the half-light, Ismael's Lada groaning under the weight of three men and a burka, khaki this time: I was expanding my range. I lifted my visor in the gloaming and the darkness cleared suddenly. I could take it off later, Tariq said, but on the road it was important to keep a low profile. The area might have spies. Some parts were off bounds to foreigners. We were enlisting the help of a specialist, someone who knew the terrain, who could help us enter the villages.

'Can you ride?' Ismael's rear mirror betrayed the mistrust in his eyes.

'I've been on a horse lots of times,' I said cheerily, though I couldn't imagine riding in a burka.

'And a camel?'

'Not really. What's it like?'

'It's more like surfing,' he said, but as Ismael had never been surfing, he wasn't exactly sure what that meant.

We fell silent then, interrupted only by the loud belly laugh of Genghis in the front seat.

We bumbled along the dusty old track. I slipped off my burka and rearranged my headscarf. It was airless beneath and I was willing to risk it.

The car popped to a premature halt. Thin, fragile children, their bare feet hennaed after the recent holy day, clambered over the bonnet, their pockets bulging with stale bread that they had gathered. The crowd of fathers nearby were oblivious of our arrival, rapt in concentration over a sort of desert draughts which was at a crucial point, dung and twigs poised at stalemate. One of them looked up, leathery hands gesticulating, and began ambling towards us. Genghis put down his rifle and translated.

The man began speaking, his face so lined it resembled a pencil sketch. He seemed impressed by my sunglasses.

'Gucci?' he asked, pointing at them.

'Boots,' I said.

'Ah, Boots!' he exclaimed.

'Please, keep them,' I said, handing them to him.

'Thank you,' he replied, taking them.

Horses, cows and goats roamed freely about the nomad encampment. Camels, like teapots, munched contentedly. All nine of them were completely different characters, he said, now looking like a film star. Hooloo was shy and timid, and had to be coaxed and chivvied. Mooz was a law unto herself. Angur was a Taliban camel. He only kicked women. Despite their idiosyncrasies, said the drover, they were easier to deal with than all three of his wives and seven children.

In reality, a nomad's life was anything but romantic. It was a fight for survival. There was no electricity, no sewage system, and no running water. The soil was poor for growing vegetables. The children had over an hour's walk to school every morning. Water was the greatest problem: it had to be carried from the river in jerry cans, litre by litre. No one begged, no one complained. Weaving and selling allowed them to scrape a living for six months a year. The rest of the year they worked in the fields and ate the vegetables they had planted, while only a few hundred miles south hotels were offering traditional hospitality in luxury nomad tents. They tried to hold on to their old traditions, baking their own bread and slaughtering their animals for meat: twenty camels, three dozen sheep and eight donkeys shared between them. Occasionally they sold one off, but only the male ones.

Beneath the low, wide goat-hair of the tent, the scent of diesel, spices, tea and burning dung weighed heavy. Ancient mothers and their daughters busied themselves with their weaving. Small carvings dangled about their colourful skirts, gold braid, and coins to guard against the evil eye, and their heads were uncovered. The rugs bore traditional patterns, but some had American flags, tanks and guns; one even showed the planes flying into the World Trade Centre on 9/11. There was a big demand for these in the export market, apparently.

They offered me green tea from a kettle. There was no food. If there had been any it would have already been on the table. Still, I hesitated before accepting. It would be impolite to refuse, but you could not take from those who already had nothing, nothing but their pride and their humanity, those things they could never have taken from them.

Mira, the drover's first wife, smiled, her frown lines cemented by affliction and time. Aziza, the second wife, was a beautiful young girl, high-cheekboned.

'Who is your prophet?' she asked me, pointing at the cross around my neck.

'Jesus,' I said.

'And is he alive?'

'He lives in hearts,' I said, pointing to mine.

The wives shared their husbands, as they shared everything. Was Hassan a good husband, I wondered. I sensed a tension as deep as their worry lines.

'*Tahamul*,' she said gravely, wrinkling a faded tribal tattoo on her forehead. Only later did Tariq explain the word. It meant 'endure'.

Outside the drover was rounding up the camels like an anxious parent, putting guide ropes into their mouths, which were green and frothy from chewing the cud. He talked about them like family, his encyclopaedic knowledge equalled only by the size of his turban. There was a long time to learn. A camel was not just for Eid, it was for life, it seemed. They lived until they were sixty.

Genghis effortlessly jumped up on Hooloo, and Tariq climbed on Angur, who honked in protest before giving a menacing hiss. When asked to walk, he stopped and chewed, and no profanity in any language, no amount of chivvying, heel-digging or kicking, could move him on. I myself clambered on Mooz who, with a gruff snort, turned her head. With a flirtatious bat of the eyelashes, Mooz pitched me forward. I immediately fell off, landing smartly on my bottom. It was only at the third try that I managed to hang on, and it was with all the effort I could muster. The men found it hilarious. Even the nomads were chuckling uncontrollably.

We set off to a chorus of grunts, braying, and the clanking of caravan bells. Only the drover did not ride, preferring to walk. He would be looking out for mines, he said. Silence descended against the gentle flip-flopping of sandals and camel feet. The sure, velvety footsteps were soothing. A cloud floated in the vast hot sky, the odd parched tree drooping beneath the glare. The white line of the horizon seemed endless, broken at one stage by a caravan of laden dromedaries, rich pickings for any highway bandit. Luckily our own small train had nothing worth stealing, just a bit of bribe money, some guns, a few tatty blankets and the odd infidel.

I slapped at mosquitos. As the sand whipped my face in an unexpected emery-board facial, I raised my hands to shadow my eyes, aware of my knicker elastic climbing like a damp tendril around the top of my legs. From time to time Mooz flung her head back, violently scratching my thigh with her head. She had an itch, said the drover.

On we rode into the emptiness. Thomas Thomson, my botanical ancestor, would have been sorely disappointed; there were no desert flowers here, only the odd tuft of sagebrush or camel thorn. I had heard the East revealed its secrets so slowly that it took unending patience to discover them. Progress seemed so slow that sometimes it felt as if we were treading water. Only the landscape seemed constantly moving, formed and unformed by the wind, like the rippling waves of the sea, smooth and still, full and yet empty, magical and yet daunting, everything held in perfect balance.

At a sprawling acacia bush we took a break. The camels gathered, limbs collapsing like deck chairs, long, furry tongues tearing and stripping the thorns to get to the tiny leaves. The drover unravelled a blanket, which he positioned on the ground facing east, took a few splashes of the water from the bottle and performed his ablutions. The others joined in, and together they bowed, prayed, stood, then bowed and prayed again, four times in all, completing their invocations in perfect unison, silhouetted against the sky, bonded by their devotions. I watched, chewing on a piece of stale bread, savouring the crunchy consistency, no doubt from that special desert ingredient – sand.

The camels rose grudgingly and as we rode on, the land became harder, more barren, the sand grilled to a torrid ochre, in places fissured by the heat. The white line of the horizon faded into a mirage, an untidy line of buildings that looked as if they might be struggling to keep up with each other. There was not much to see: a motorbike, a cart, a donkey, a few men hunkering by the roadside wrapped in cloths and melancholy. We dismounted and approached.

The men who greeted us were locals, elders and holy men. Some clutched rifles so old they looked as if they had been excavated. They smiled graciously, glancing furtively in my direction as if they had never seen a woman before, and certainly not a foreign one. One of them stepped forward. Robed and turbaned, wiry of build, leaning on a grimy stick whose knob was carved into a crescent moon the same shape as the pouches under his eyes, he stared over our heads as if addressing someone not there. He was blind, whispered Ismael.

An inconspicuous doorway stood at the side of what looked like a folly, but turned out to be a pigeon tower, castellated and with elaborate brickwork. Inside grapes lay drying, strung on the wall upon slats. There were no windows, just a hole issuing a blast of hot dust. We sat down cross-legged, the two groups eyeing each other, the blind man leaning forward and listening intently. As Tariq extended a few notes, he turned his face towards them as if he had smelt them. He put out his hand for them, felt them, and nodded.

Genghis passed round the photograph of Zaki, and the men shook their heads in bafflement. No, there was no one of that name in their village, they said. Yes, yes, they were certain; of course they would have known. They knew everyone in the village by name. Again he asked, repeating the name, and more bewildered looks and doubtful glances were exchanged.

'Dostum told you he was here?' asked the old man.

'Not exactly. It was one of his men who told us to come here.'

'And who was this man?'

'He did not give his name.'

'What did he look like, this hostage?' asked the blind man.

'Not bad,' said Tariq, 'for an Uzbek, that is . . .'

'Uzbek?' he echoed. 'I would have known.'

'You have not heard from the General, then?' asked Genghis, coming to the point.

'Dostum?' said the old man, somewhat baffled at the question.

'Yes, Dostum, or one of his men?'

The old man shook his head. 'It is complicated,' he said gravely. The war was complicated. Everything was. . .

'Yes,' agreed Tariq. There was no denying it.

We made our excuses, and left the man to turn his blind eye to what had turned out to be another blind alley. All this way for nothing, whispered Tariq, as we rode off in the fading light. We were all in the darkness now.

In the distance, plumes rose from the fires in the camp, orange dots in a sea of cobalt, beacons of hope. There was not a breath of wind. Shoots of brightness streamed among the stars, but they were motionless. A rising star never appeared to be moving. It gave always the illusion of stillness, the shadow of its brightness barely discernible. In the mottled shadows playing on the sand, I imagined pictures, echoes of home, faces of those dear to me. I scanned them for missing connections, destinations it seemed we would never reach. Like the line of the horizon, they were beyond us.

Home at last the camels collapsed. I tucked cash in the saddles, and avoided the rears. As we parted the drover begged me hold out my hand. Into it he placed an egg, still warm and smooth, smelling of earth and dung. I wrapped it in a handkerchief, wondering what to do with it.

Ismael smiled his bright smile when he saw the egg. It was free-range, he said, like the nomads. He would cook it for breakfast.

★ ☽ ★

That egg was delicious, and there was another delight in store for us before we left. Ismael had something to show us. It was not far and was on the way to the airport. It was worth the detour. Soon a building glistened like a mirage, framed by a sprawling mass of low-lying mud cubes that seemed to set it off to advantage. White doves flocked round it like snowflakes. On the marble flagstones people gathered, wailing and praying, waiting to be healed and blessed, men on one side, women and children cordoned off behind them. Gazar Gah meant 'the Bleaching Ground', a place where pilgrims could cleanse their souls before Allah. It was one of Afghanistan's holiest sites, dedicated to the saint and poet Khoja Abdulla Ansari. Ismael hoped we could cleanse our souls, too. Pure souls would mean we could not fail in our mission to save Zaki.

Outside the dome, cross-legged holy men read from the Qur'an, bowing in reverence. A craftsman knelt on one leg, the other tucked in front of him. Bent in concentration, he was chinking away beside a pile of glazed lozenges in yellow, lapis, brown and white, each tile with a scrap of paper glued on to the front indicating where he should cut. It looked as though there were thousands – no, hundreds of thousands. 'Nearly there,' he said with a smile.

We took off our shoes and the men surrendered their rifles. As the entrance guard waved at me, I wondered whether he was waving me in or wafting the smell away. Tariq suspected he was waving me out, but we ignored him anyway and went on in.

And what an inside it was. We strained our necks at the incredible tile work. The configurations of pattern were dizzying, made in intricate mosaic, the motifs based on ancient designs with all their coded secrets. Blue bands of inscriptions from the Qur'an framed the arches and panels. In some places, the complexity felt overwhelming; in others the simplicity of line, shade and light was luminous. Swirly turquoise vines with tendrils and tiny flowers, or

CHAPTER 19

'Two Watermelons Cannot be Held In One Hand'

دو تربوز به یک دست گرفته نمی شود .

'Is that *it*?' said Omar.

'Yes!' I cried ecstatically. I dived out of the car with such gusto my veil came off.

Caught off guard, the dog froze in terror. She put out her front paws a little and her lip flickered in a pitiful whine. I studied her carefully. She was filthier, thinner and more dejected than ever, the wound on her neck still raw, the same abject sorrow in her eyes, but there was no doubt she was the one. Gently, slowly, I put my hand on the flank. Another little pat, and she turned round and looked at me. Then she opened her mouth and howled.

I sat down in the dirt and pondered. It wasn't exactly a question of logic or foresight. As with so many important decisions, in that moment the solution felt entirely natural, as if you already knew it, though if anyone had asked you to explain yourself you wouldn't have been able to. You inevitably looked back and saw what a fool you'd been. If only you hadn't been so impulsive and reckless, you could have thought it through properly, made the right decision, and saved yourself and others a lot of bother. I wondered what my father would have done. He loved dogs, but was not given to sentimentality. He would have analysed it logically, recognising the pitfalls, listing the absurdities of becoming involved – and in a foreign country, no less. But then, I was not my father. For me it was a gut decision, a reflex. There was no doubt in my mind that this was a gentle dog. There was something of nobility about her. I couldn't let her die.

I stood up, dusted myself down, and walked in to the reception desk. In the spirit of old-fashioned tact and diplomacy I put my case calmly but firmly. 'No dogs allowed in any circumstances!' snapped the hotel manager. I tried again, this time even more firmly, fixing him with my gaze, recklessly abandoning my female modesty. But it was clear that no amount of pleading or supplication was going to make the slightest difference. The manager waved his arms in dismissal.

'It's either both of us or neither,' I insisted. But even when I thrust a bank note into his hand, it had no effect. He just huffed and puffed, slammed his book shut, and gazed into the distance as if I weren't there. There was nothing for it but subterfuge.

Smuggling the dog up the stairs turned out to be much easier than I had expected. I had visions of squeezing the poor creature into my carpetbag, muzzle poking out of the top, but when it came to it, I simply picked her up and carried her. The manager had disappeared and the guards at the entrance were so engrossed in chatting and smoking that the dog and I slipped up unnoticed. In my room I made a bed of clean clothes upon filthy blankets, carefully avoiding the multiple electrocution opportunities of the bathroom. The dog, limp and bewildered, gave a cursory sniff and, like a shy houseguest not wanting to intrude, cowered in the corner. I put down some water and she drank a little, but she seemed too exhausted even to lap efficiently. The head bowed, the body curled, the eyes closed.

An hour or so passed as she slept, whimpering in dream talk, feet jerking as if running away from something. I had no idea what I was doing either. Suddenly the dog started, pricked up her ears and opened her eyes. Wearily she lifted her bony legs. She faltered a bit and sat back down. At the second attempt she stood, a little wobbly, lifting her head to greet the day as if there was new hope in it. I opened the door, trying hard to stifle the squeak it made in closing. As I tiptoed downstairs with my holdall, no one noticed the damp, whiskery muzzle peeking out from the zip, nor heard the faint scufflings from within.

At the end of the street the traffic was at a standstill. Beggars limped in and around the stationary lanes like artful dodgers. In the middle of the jam Omar was banging his horn amid a chorus of others. There was no point parking at the side of the street, he said, because the whole street was a car park, so he might as well stay in the middle. I carefully stepped round a donkey and gratefully into the back seat. As the traffic moved we edged on gradually, and when I draped my scarf over the lumpy object that protruded from the top of the bag, he didn't bat an eyelid.

'Do you know any rooms I could rent?' I said. 'I am homeless.'

Omar gestured wildly. 'I have perfect place,' he announced cheerily. 'It is a *special* place, a secret place, a safe place, the best in all Afghanistan!'

'*Khoob*, good,' I said gratefully. Whatever the cost, whatever the risk, it would be fine.

★ ☽ ★

I was not to be disappointed. It was a broken sort of building, wrapped in a mantle of decay. What remained listed slightly, as if the plaster itself were on crutches. The noise from the street lingered by its torn walls, where a few turbaned men were leaning as if to prop them up. The sky was bright, but when the eye looked down shadows lurked inside. Yet something was drifting to brighten the gloom. A scent lingered, mingled with the usual scent. It was smoky and sweet. It was the unmistakable aroma of fresh, baking *naan*.

Inside soft cushions of dough billowed on a stone bench the length of the wall. Small boys with dark, clear eyes that dominated their faces yelled commands in treble voices. One broke off lumps from the dough mass and shaped them into balls; another kneaded and rolled them into ovals, putting a pattern on them with a roller. He took the rolled dough and tossed it across the backs of his hands until it expanded and thinned out. Then he threw it on to a domed cushion, slipped his hand into a pocket at the back of the cushion and slapped it on to the scorching wall inside the oven, where it began to bubble and turn golden. Then a third boy, armed with a long rod and a metal hook, pulled off the bread and flicked it through an opening. All the while a fourth used a rusty set of bellows to fan the fire beneath the circular *tandoor*, the clay oven.

The baker emerged. Short and slight, with the face of a prophet, he wiped his brow with the tail of his turban. 'How are you keeping?' I asked him. 'Pain, loss, death . . . the usual,' he said. How could anyone think straight about anything, when all they could think about was their empty bellies? If it wasn't one thing it was another: the weather, the politics, the women. The cost of wheat flour had shot up in the past three months. Last year the crop had failed, and flour had had to be transported over the mountains, smuggled in by children who made the journey to earn just a few *afghanis*. I asked him about a room, and he paused and thought for a moment, stroking his beard and nodding. He extended his large palm, smiling, and as I dutifully greased it, his eyes lit up. So delighted was he at the prospect of a steady rent that he was only too pleased to turn a blind eye to the black ones that stared out from the holdall I was carrying. He handed me the key and grinned.

The great key was painted yellow to make it look like gold. Shakily I entered it in the lock where it wobbled mournfully. It was largely redundant. A great hole in the door would let anyone in and out as they wished. I left my shoes at the spot where others had left theirs and crept shoeless over the dusty floorboards. In the pale gloom within I noticed the falls of cobwebs, the crawlings of spiders, the tracks and droppings of mice, and even fainter ones of beetles and their families. At the back lay a paved yard and a little garden sadly devoid of plants, except for an attempt to train some creeping shrubs and to make a small fountain, which was dry, in a grotto decorated with a statue, which was gone. At the top of the steps lay a door so intricately carved it took my breath away.

The dog jumped out and vanished immediately. I stepped across the dull, slippery floor, glancing around, noticing the details, the picture of Mecca, the gaudy vase with artificial flowers, two artificial butterflies hovering above on sticks, the flat cushions, the bed (as usual too short), the mattress too thin, the gas primus and oil lamp. Then there was the draped doorway, the hole in the floor, tap and water tank, unfilled as usual. It felt like a good moment to call someone.

It was a fact that Tariq hated dogs. Dogs were bad, dogs were dirty, dogs, above all, were against the Faith. The Prophet preferred cats. I hesitated at first, but Genghis was not answering, and neither were the women. So I steeled myself and rang him. I broke it to him, gently at first, then firmly, as a *fait accompli*. I knew there was going to be trouble and there was – the lice, the ticks, the responsibility. Allah Almighty! Had the girl totally lost her senses?

Twenty minutes later he was there on the doorstep, Maryam behind him with a great bag of biscuits and an armful of *naan*. We bent down, put the bread in the centre of the room and waited.

'Come on,' purred Maryam. 'Come on,' echoed her brother softly. Still the dog refused to budge. With thumb and forefinger Maryam pulled out a chunk of bread from the bag, placed it on the biscuits and nudged it closer to the sniffing sounds. Suddenly a black nose poked forward, sniffing, just the tip at first, then a whisker, a muzzle, and finally the whole head. 'She's gorgeous!' said Maryam, as the mass of fur emerged from the shadows.

'Her breath stinks!' cried Tariq, trying to look disgruntled, but as he turned away he failed to convince either of us. I could tell that he liked her.

★ ☽ ★

Some scraps of meat and crusts of bread, and soon there came a change. We decided to call her *Gurgak*. It meant 'little wolf'. Maryam visited often during those days. She brought ointment for Little Wolf's cuts, strange lotions for her fleas, and helped with the bathing, massaging the sudsy bubbles into her back, steadying the torso with soothing words while we dried the paws, stroking the head, taking the warm towel and rubbing. Tariq, though he pretended disinterest, was equally smitten, and Little Wolf seemed unafraid as she lifted her head and sniffed him. Fussing wore her out, but she seemed too polite to resist. Any sudden noise or movement would still send her into apoplexy. At night her frail body sent still out waves of unhappiness as she slept, shuddering involuntarily from time to time.

In the morning she would whine in alarm until she opened her eyes and I comforted her. Bravely she would edge nearer the bed, bunching up next to me, keeping a vigil between me and the door. At others she seemed to settle, bravely placing her nose in my hand, scraping her teeth against the biscuits, softening every morsel in her mouth, discovering a hundred new flavours and savouring every bite. I allowed her to work me out gradually, understanding when she needed to make a crotch sniff, allowing her to smell me as much as she wanted, offering an open hand.

With regular food and blankets to sleep on, Little Wolf slowly began to relax, as if she was too sick and tired to be wild any more. Gradually the episodes of shaking ebbed and the sore on her neck began healing. More and more she allowed us to touch her. Slowly we encouraged her to take exercise, letting her out in the yard where the weeds flourished under her attention. She ate anything we fed to her, and even began chewing the carpet.

Tariq, I could see, was warming to her. What better world of fun for a dog than a walk, he said one day, almost caringly. There would be ants and birds and other creatures to follow and be interested in. There was the sun to hunt as it stole through the leaves of the cypress, and a thousand scents on the summer breeze, and water to lap and splash about in.

So we marked his steps through the crowds to the sidecar, and suddenly there we were, squashed together: one foreigner, one dog, and one disgruntled Afghan at the wheel, with moustache, scarf, and ears human and canine flapping in the wind. The sidecar popped and bumped along a road that crept up a hillside strewn with rubbish. With Little Wolf stuffed on my lap, *eau de chien* mingled with *Agent Provocateur* perfume in a suffocating cocktail. As we screeched to a halt, all three of us were bouleversé from the stench and the shock.

Tariq strode off at such a pace that neither dog nor I were able to keep up with him. Little Wolf walked tentatively, whimpering softly, and so we let him go ahead. I threw a stick, and she looked blank, resting her head wearily upon a front paw, so I fetched it myself, and after a few such runs collapsed exhausted. Then, as I sat down beside her in the dust, she rolled over, and as we bathed in the sunlight, I closed my eyes and checked myself. How could the sun shine so brightly when all the world was tumbling? I tried to picture my family, but the details of their faces blurred and faded.

Tariq dropped us home after another hair-raising ride in the sidecar, and Little Wolf followed me up the stairs in silence, devouring the meat and bread I put down for her, and, although I had told her a million times not to, peeing confidently into the corner of the room. Happy at last, she fell asleep.

From then on she seemed to enjoy our walks together. In the labyrinth of mud-walled alleys, a dog's nose proved the best map of all. There were many distractions en route, so we would go a bit, then rest, dither slightly, and often give up altogether. At those times I would gently guide her outside the bakery to the dog-sized hole in the front door where she knew she could go inside and find food, water and shelter. I would then draw the scarf across my face and head off alone again.

I worried constantly for her. At all times I felt I was just borrowing her company. She was a wild dog, after all, a free spirit that would never be tamed. Any human she met was bound to be a passing influence, at worst an enemy, at best a friend, but never a master. I tried to make her understand that humans were not all hostile, and that she was free to leave at any time, on her own terms; in response she would sit, tongue wagging, staring at me blankly, refusing to budge. Fortunately the hole in the front door served as a makeshift dog flap, allowing her to come and go whenever she wanted to pee or wander; and the flexibility of this arrangement seemed for a few days to be working rather well. She would disappear regularly, before suddenly appearing again, usually at dusk or when cooking smells were in the air. It was at those times I loved her most.

★ ☽ ★

With all this in mind, it was only a matter of time before the inevitable happened. It was one of those evenings that fell so lightly it was barely there, around about sunset, the hour when, it was said by Muslims, the gates of heaven were opened, the gates of hell closed, and Satan put into chains.

We had set off in good spirits, Little Wolf and I, wandering the sandy maze of alleyways that were deeper and richer in the golden light, the dog following purpose-fully. Soldiers stared blankly at us, as Little Wolf caught a whiff of them. The dog held her own for a moment, body stiffening, ears flattening, fur rising on her back. Then, sensing defeat, she rolled over.

We pressed on to another set of passageways, wrecked buildings and hordes of busy people. A street-seller was shouting his wares. Little Wolf went into overdrive, wagging her tail, whimpering with excitement. I bought a *sheer yakh*, an ice-cream, licked it and gave the rest up; and as she gobbled it whole I could swear I saw her smiling.

Further along the street, we halted suddenly, stopped in our tracks by a bang. As I looked upwards, one of the houses seemed to be heaving, its outer wall surging forward. A storm of dust was snowing in a million tumbling fragments. Choked and blinded, I hid my face as the buried memory came flooding back – of the day in the square I had tried to forget, the day of the bus bombing. A few ghostly faces, whitened with the fallout, appeared, shouting. They looked numbed, perhaps from the shock or from blows they had received from falling wood and plaster. I turned round, and to my horror the dog had gone.

'Little Wolf!' I called out again and again, but the dog with no name didn't know its new one. I searched frantically through the crowded street. Nothing. I pressed on, to the next street, and the next, taking no more notice of the throng than a sleepwalker. Still no sign of her. On I went, weaving recklessly through the traffic jam alongside the beggars. I enquired of people: the guards at the park, the police at the checkpoints, the street-sellers, the hotel-keepers, the queues of sick standing outside the hospital, a phone-card seller, an old man with a donkey.

The narrow streets of the old city proved no more fruitful. I punched the keys of my phone, but it was dead. I was holding in the tears, hurrying across the streets as if trying to find somewhere to hide them. Distraught, I sat down on the bare ground and sobbed my heart out. It was several hours later in darkness that I finally made it back to the bakery.

★ ☽ ★

The following morning we divided the map into quarters, and set off in different directions, Tariq muttering and swearing, Genghis resigned, Maryam and I resolved. We had decided to dispense with our burkas. What was the point in searching for something when we couldn't see properly?

In the rush to get ready a few stray strands of red hair peeped out disobediently from my headscarf, and as I pushed them back it seemed to me I was attracting more eyes than ever. Street merchants stared, busy burkas slackened their pace, and turned their heads. I didn't care. There was only one thing on my mind – Little Wolf.

Failing in our attempts in the first area we renewed them in another, until eventually we were back to where we had begun in the centre of the bazaar. A row of goat heads strung up by a butcher's stall, like trophies of medieval torture. There were piles of sheep heads and fish strung up in lines. Men hacked at carcasses with iron axes over wooden stumps, and an audience was gathering.

I swung around and in that split second lost sight of Maryam. A strange sensation of panic filled me now. She couldn't be far, could she? But as I strained to see over the bobbing heads of the crowd, the faces, once smiling, now seemed hostile. With Maryam out of sight, I peeked round tentatively, curious to know what spectacle was enthralling them, then immediately regretted it.

Already the hind legs of a lamb were being bound and the struggling animal wrestled to the ground. A man dressed in a violet overcoat invoked the name of Allah as he whipped a smooth blade swiftly across the lamb's throat. Frozen, I watched as the bulbous eyes stared wildly, the bushy tail swishing to and fro. My instinct to scream was overtaken by the numbness of shock, and I was unable to move. The scrawny legs began to twitch, and made desperate scurrying movements. I wondered if the creature was conscious, if it was in pain. There seemed no mistaking that it was. Seconds later it let out long sigh, followed by a sobbing death rattle as the head fell gently to the ground, blood gushing thickly from the wound. Then the tail stopped twitching. After it was all over, the butcher uttered a blessing before moving swiftly to cut the lamb into two in one clean cut, the hook tearing into its still-warm flesh.

Disorientated by the eruption of blood and the staring faces, I crossed the street, still searching for Maryam, aware of the soft ground crumbling, not noticing my tunic snagging and ripping around me. The horizon was descending and then rising again. Around, voices seemed to address me as if they came from somewhere else. I felt hot and sick, and nearly fell over. 'I'm most terribly sorry,' I said in English, 'I think I'm going to lie down.' The rest was just a blur.

★ ☽ ★

For several days the fever went on, though I myself lost track of time. An hour might have been a minute, an afternoon a day. I was conscious of the oddest things: the variations in the light, the shape of the room, an object at the side of the bed, the ripples and dimples in the wall, of being cold and then burning again, and the chirrup of a songbird. My throat was engorged, dotted with canker sores that made it painful to swallow. I was sweating, gasping almost, under the pressure of trying to breathe, and I was delirious. The colour of the room faded. Different permutations of the human face would hover over me, then would evaporate again, settling into one I knew but couldn't place. The darkness deepened, its blue-black seeping like emptiness, and then nothing.

A figure appeared to be bending over me, holding my hand. At first I thought it was my mother, smiling kindly, telling me everything was going to be all right. The image subsided, and in the background were fragments of a song, a breeze. I passed out in exhaustion again, rolling my head on the pillow, and woke with the sense of people moving about the room. Gradually I came to my senses, my body damp in a crush of coarse material, eyes blinking at the ceiling. I became aware of the presence again, leaning over and saying something. With the imprint of lips lingering softly on my cheek, the pain in my throat seemed to lessen, and I wondered for a moment whether I was still dreaming. What began as a whisper faded as soon as it passed my lips. No, it was not a ghost. It was Maryam.

Maryam laid her head on the pillow by my side and stayed there without speaking. It was wonderful that she had come, but part of me wished she hadn't. She had too much else to think about and I feared she would catch the virus. As the mist of my senses began clearing, I swallowed and a searing pain cut through the back of my throat. Her face came close again, as she placed her hand behind my head, taking a glass to my mouth, urging me to drink.

'How long have I . . . ?' I gasped.

'Don't think of that now. Just rest.'

I was falling again, head slumping back on the pillow. When I woke once more there was no light other than that of the fire, which cast a flicker on the face that looked like shadow. On wakening again I glanced about the room, which seemed unchanged from before, except for the roses by my bed, which had wilted, falling in a tangle of stems and thorns.

'Wait there,' said Maryam, and disappeared.

The door creaked and my heart skipped as I saw Little Wolf as if for the first time, wagging, panting, sniffing and kissing, letting out a bark of happiness.

'How did you find her?' I cried.

'It's a long story,' said Tariq. 'And there is something else . . .'

'What's that?'

'We are going to have babies!'

For a second my face crumpled with confusion, before Maryam pointed to the dog.

Little Wolf rolled over to reveal a row of resplendent teats, her abdomen swollen slightly. That look in her eyes told me all I needed to know. It was the look of love.

CHAPTER 20

'He Eats Tail Fat with the Wolf and Cries with the Shepherd'

دزد را بگویند دزدی کن و صاحبِ خانه را بگویند خبردار

I came out of the fever vowing never again to touch Afghan ice-cream, and, after witnessing that slaughter, I had become an instant vegetarian. Although my stomach was settling and my head and throat healing, images I tried to forget still haunted me. What was worse, Zaki was still missing. The officials remained cagey as to whether they knew anything at all about it, and our momentum was slackening. We worried now, that he might be presumed dead, and forgotten. And, after so long without news, even the family now began to wonder if it was worth the effort.

Ahmed was, perhaps unsurprisingly, the most ardent opponent to our efforts. The wedding was never going to happen, he argued; no one would blame us if we called it off. Sohaila, too, had become despondent. For her, the whole family's future was at stake, not just Maryam's. In her eyes there were plenty of suitors where Zaki came from. If he wasn't coming back it was better to accept it now. Tariq remained philosophical. We had come this far, he said; Allah would not desert us. Genghis agreed with him, but wondered if Allah was having a little joke with us. Of all of us, Maryam was the bravest, never for a second losing hope. Underneath we could tell she was suffering. Her mother made her *laytee* to warm her, a sort of spicy custard, but nothing could combat the sleeplessness.

I myself, felt helpless. What had begun so long ago as an inquiry into a different culture had become a duty of friendship, and that duty had taken yet another twist. My presence here was now about honour, something as important to me as it was to the Afghans, who held the concept as dear as their devotion to prayer. The prospect of letting my friends down was unthinkable. I had given my word to help them, and I intended to keep my promise, whatever it cost me.

★ ☽ ★

In the dim light of the bakery room we gathered round the maps again, scratching our heads and yawning, Genghis twiddling his moustache with an upward motion, Tariq stroking his non-existent one. Maryam looked exhausted, drumming her hand on the weave of the carpet. Half-heartedly I cut a pomegranate. The sweet taste left a tinge of acid on my tongue. As the sticky seeds spilled out on my chin it felt now, for the first time, as if we had all finally reached our limit.

Little Wolf was nowhere to be seen, but this time she hadn't run away; she had just crept under the bed. A while later she poked her nose out at the bag of scraps that Tariq had brought round for her. Then, having boldly gulped a few pieces, barely chewing before she swallowed, she retreated contentedly, with a full belly and a nice dark refuge. Snuffling noises were soon audible. At first they sounded like snoring, but as I listened to the noise again I realised the sound was coming from somewhere else. It was hard to make out what it was exactly. You might have called it a hubbub. It seemed to abate, then start up again and grow louder, until finally we could clearly discern a shout, like a donkey's braying, followed by rattling at the door below. Little Wolf, excited, began barking from her hideout. Who could it be, we all wondered.

I hurried to the window. As I peering down at the street, it was only now that I saw it, the wide and towering turban that could belong to only one person. As the figure turned, I was not to be disappointed. The Mullah slowly raised his head and smiled. He followed me up the stairs panting, his difficulty in breathing, he said, heightened by his frustration at the traffic.

We all exchanged our courtesies, before settling down cross-legged on the floor.

'I bring news that might interest you,' huffed our visitor, casting his eye about the room disapprovingly.

'What have you come to tell us?' ventured Tariq impatiently.

'Well,' spluttered the Mullah, still panting from the climb, 'first, I must have your word of confidence . . .'

'By Allah, you have it,' we said as one.

'Well then,' he said, having collected himself. 'The General, who I have known for many years, as a boy and then a man . . .'

'What about him?'

'He was talking with someone . . .'

'Who was it?'

'It would not be wise . . .' he sighed, as a cluster of eyes fell disappointed from his gaze.

'The point is, I believe, the young gentleman you have been seeking . . .'

'Yes?'

'. . . is not exactly dead,' said the Mullah.

'He is not in Herat,' snapped Tariq.

'May I take you into my confidence?' said the Mullah enthusiastically.

'Of course,' sighed Genghis.

An exchange of confidences ensued that went too fast for me to understand. Then something jumped out. As the Mullah spoke the word in Dari I couldn't help repeating it in English.

'*Kaftar* . . .'

'Pigeon?' said Tariq, wrinkling his nose. '*Kaftar*? Perhaps you mean *kaftaar*?' he said, stressing the last syllable. The two words were almost the same, it turned out, but the pronunciation varied, as did the meaning.

'A dog?' I was a little confused now.

'A hyena . . .'

'A hyena?' I was staring at him blankly. They didn't have hyenas in Afghanistan, did they?

'Actually it's neither,' said the Mullah. '*Kaftar* is a name.'

'A person?' Maryam was gazing at him wide-eyed.

With renewed vigour he started off again, sneaking wistful gazes at me that filled me with unease.

'A person known to Dostum . . .'

'And is Dostum going to help us with this . . . er . . . person?' asked Tariq.

'That depends,' said the Mullah craftily.

'On what?'

'I would be prepared to put in a word if . . .'

'If what?'

'If you would reconsider my very fortunate proposal?' said the Mullah, glancing at me sideways. 'I knew I had been right to tell you,' he added smugly. 'I am an obliging man and never wish to disappoint. My helpful reputation is legendary, and I had a duty to fulfil my role as intermediary. No one can accuse me of not having tried my best which, as a great man, I invariably have.'

The time had come for straight talking. 'Thank you,' I said flatly, 'but I'm afraid I have no intention of marrying at all.'

Purple with irritation, the Mullah took a cigarette from Genghis's fingers and began smoking it. Soon afterwards he wrapped his shawl around his shoulders, rose to his feet, and in no time had merged into the shadows outside.

With water on the stove to boil for a fresh pot of tea, cardamom and sugar poised, Genghis dialled a number. Nothing. Another attempt, and silence again. Then, out of nowhere, came a breakthroug with news that was as enlightening as it was terrifying. Kaftar, said Genghis after the conversation had ended, was well known in the province of Baghlan. Kaftar had a private army and a penchant for bloodletting. All was not lost, however. Zaki's life could be bought, but if payment was not made they would almost certainly kill him.

'How much do they want then?' asked Tariq.

'Fifty thousand . . .'

'*Afghanis*?'

'Dollars.'

'Dollars!' I wailed. I turned out my purse and we watched the few traveller's cheques fluttering down like feathers.

'That,' said Tariq flatly, 'is not enough.'

'Maybe it's not just about the money,' said Maryam defiantly.

'It's always about the money,' sighed Genghis.

'Will they negotiate?'

'I don't know,' said Tariq. 'We'll just have to try.'

'And is this person – has he Taliban friends?' I gulped.

'Not sure . . .' muttered Tariq.

A protracted silence followed. Then Genghis's eyes lit up suddenly.

'Do you want to share a glass of *doagh* with us?' he wondered at last. It was a local drink that would put hairs on my chest and iron in my belly. Politely I declined. I had a feeling it had yoghurt in it.

'*Parendagak*, little bird,' he purred then, stroking his whiskers and lowering his great, dark eyes on me, 'do you believe in destiny?'

I bit my lip and nodded. Of course I did, I told him, and as he strode urgently out of the room vowing to be back later, I knew this was my date with it.

A whimper. Some scratchings. Something was stirring under the bed again. Little Wolf, who had been oblivious of the drama, poked her nose out from her hidey-hole, gave a cursory sniff, ears revolving like satellite dishes. She picked herself up and strolled out of the door. We all admitted it was a welcome distraction.

An uneasy hour passed while we twiddled our thumbs. Tariq was upbeat as he began his normal pacing up and down the room. At last we were getting somewhere, he said. Didn't he tell us Allah was helping us? Didn't he say he would never desert us? Grateful as I was for any supernatural assistance in our situation, as I saw it our options were limited. To secure Dostum's support, I would have to pander to the Mullah. Alternatively I would have to sell most of my possessions to afford it. It was either prostitution or destitution, and probably both.

It felt like an age before Genghis returned in a blast of sandalwood. He sat on the carpet, hatching something, adding his own spin. 'Plan' was a not wholly accurate way of describing it. It felt more like Russian roulette.

Several pints of tea later we were all in agreement. To reach the kidnappers we would first need to meet with an intermediary, who would require an extra back-hander. It was the usual drill, he said matter-of-factly. They would not divulge the whereabouts of this person nor give his name over the telephone. We were to go to the Ghazni Stadium and be given directions from there. If we valued Zaki's life we would have to show ourselves to be co-operating. Genghis would act as our emissary. He was, after all, armed and huge and, if you didn't know him, very scary.

I decided to go with him. It was, after all, my money he was dishing out, but we all knew that was an excuse. I couldn't help thinking that it would be a pity to miss out on the action now that things were finally hotting up. Resistance was futile. After the usual protestations I was pleased to find everyone gave in surprisingly quickly. As I promised to keep on my burka, I knew that was the easy bit. Staying silent, just like an Afghan woman, was the tallest order of all.

The following morning we first headed to the bank, one hulking bear of a figure and one incognito burka nestling under his wing. We then took Genghis's jeep, and parked outside the stadium. Genghis wished a group of guards a happy day, and as I slunk silently in his wake, it felt strange and unnerving. The contact was waiting for us. Genghis gave his usual thumbs-up sign, though the tone in his voice was uneasy. They had made him swear an oath of honour and secrecy, as if our lives depended on it, which they did. For a moment it seemed all to be off. Then, eventually the tone calmed, and a time and an address were mentioned. Genghis handed over the money, and the man's car sped off. I rubbed at the goose bumps on my arm, relieved my frightened face was concealed by the burka.

On the pitch nostrils were flaring, equine and human. Hooves were thundering and whips lashing. *Buzkashi* was a national pastime, but it looked like chaos. The horses in the mêlée bunched up, before thinning out again, to frenzied encouragement from the crowd. Occasionally a few heads could be discerned in the haze, riders hanging precariously above their mounts or dangling off them, balancing on silver stirrups. At the perimeter, thousands of men were screaming and cheering, while a solitary loudspeaker on a pole blared out accelerated Dari. A handsome grey came pounding from among the rest. His rider lifted something to his saddle and clung on to it. It was a dead goat, said Genghis, grinning charmingly.

As the dust cleared I made out bare patches, burnt

places still bare from where drugs had been set alight in public.

But it was the other place, large and darkly stained, where grass still refused to grow, that was the darkest. It was the place of execution, where women were shot by the Taliban for adultery.

★ ☽ ★

Makroyan lay to the north of the city. Tenement buildings rose from the dust like concrete monsters, dreary versions of 1960s Eastern European blocks. Posters hung from ruined buildings, proclaiming candidates for the forthcoming elections, puppet MPs with squeaky-clean backgrounds, bribed by the war lords to stand on their behalf. Beside the photos were slogans for safety, freedom, and justice, and symbols such as a candle or an eye, which were used on the ballot forms for the illiterate. Not that they would be voting: the Taliban made sure of that.

Children bore water and carried sacks on their heads, refugees from the cities of Pakistan who had returned to find their homes buckled. Old men with hennaed beards sat on benches of concrete smashed by war. Some whispered Allah's names; others, motionless, leant on sticks. They gazed into the distance, as if it was their sanctuary. They didn't seem to notice the children playing with plastic guns in the rubble. Neither did they bat an eyelid as our car drew up beside them.

Tariq had already arrived and was waiting outside. 'You have thirty minutes, then we're coming in,' he said hastily. Genghis nodded.

Beyond a steep, cracked stairwell framed by lines hung with washing lay a narrow doorway, where the smell of fear mingled with rotting cabbage. Climbing the nine flights was a cardiovascular workout, the concrete hard beneath my tread, the rush of adrenalin like that before an exam – only I didn't have my lucky Gonk. Above, soldiers stared down like gargoyles, AK–47s slung over their shoulders. I attempted faltering greetings. 'Salaam aleikum, peace be with you!' I said to the first soldier. 'Manda na bashi, may you not be tired,' I said to the second. 'Jor bashi, may your body prosper,' I said to the third, too late realising I shouldn't have addressed them at all.

The apartment within was stuffy, the room narrow. The hangings by the windows drooped, and dust lay thick in their ragged folds. A few nimble spiders dropped from the ceilings and scurried in and out of the crevices in the bare walls. On a cloth lay dishes containing sweets and almonds, some Nescafé and another familiar jar – who would have thought the Taliban drank Ovaltine?

The tall bristly-bearded man in the hallway had a face so drawn that it seemed to fade into the paleness of his clothing, which was all white apart from a light grey waistcoat. With his marked stoop he looked elderly, and his dark eyes framed by round gold spectacles gave him an air of wisdom that seemed beyond his modest years.

The man walked to the window, moved the curtain aside a little and peered out into the street, where two cars were waiting. He sat down in a tatty chair, glancing beyond me as if he were searching for something. Then his face brightened, glowing with what the Afghans called *afghanyar*. He looked forward to a time of peace and welcomed the reconstruction, he said in perfect English.

There seemed no good moment to raise the subject of the kidnap, and at first we avoided it. It would be bad manners to ask about it straight away. You had to broach the point gradually, unfurling it like a carpet. That was the Afghan way. Our recognition of this was a good thing, as the tall man seemed determined to tell his tale. He spoke of faith and of love, of a childhood of poverty, of his memories as a young boy eager to learn, and of the Taliban who had given him schooling and later a job in the government. With their help he had studied the Qur'an at a *madrasa*. Afterwards he had studied banking and worked as a book-keeper. He had nothing to do with the Taliban now, he said slowly, and when it came to politics he was not out to convince us or anyone. He wanted a quiet life.

His speech was faltering slightly, his words soft as he talked about his term in prison. Still he refused to name the crimes he was accused of. He was innocent of all of them. Sometimes he looked down, his gaze introspective, at others he stared listlessly at the walls as he had been so used to doing. The secret prisons in these parts were the worst, he said: the 24-hour noise, the enforced nudity, the extreme heat and cold, the verbal abuse, the sexual humiliation. There were no windows. His cell stank of excrement and urine. Cursing, punching and kicking were constant. He had been blindfolded, his hands and feet tied with electric cables. In his dark hours, he would find the freedoms that no one could take from him: those inside his head. He would carve markings on the walls with his fingernails to pass the time, and eventually the etchings covered every inch of space. He would try to remember an envelope in his palm. He opened it eagerly, but as he looked inside, his face fell again. He whispered words I did not quite catch and then we left him. On the way down the rickety staircase the guards were still staring, but my heart had stopped pounding. This time it just bled, for a freedom won that seemed not worth fighting for.

CHAPTER 21

'You Ran out From Under a Leaking Roof and Sat in the Rain'

از طلگک بزیر باران نشتن

Beyond Kabul University, to the south-west of the city, lay highways to Ghazni and Kandahar that were controlled by the Taliban, forbidden to foreigners and a death trap for Afghans. The district that provided the access to these roads was unknown to me. Rocket-fire had taken its toll on many of the buildings in Kotayi Sangi. There were the usual piles of rubble, shards of glass, bits of bombs, mangled and torn metal scrap, and unexploded grenades. Uniformed guards stood in observation towers, their faces obscured by cigarette smoke. On the ground coils of barbed wire and army camouflage netting marked the path towards checkpoints, and women laden with groceries wearily made their way past the inspection areas.

I was not sure whom we were meeting, and even when we met them I wasn't sure I would be able to make them out through my burka. Part of me felt paralysed with fear, but another part was curious, and though I hated to admit it, excited even. Were they Taliban? Were they criminals? Were they terrorists? My mind was boggling.

Tariq seemed equally uncertain, *jihad* being a grey area these days. He put it another way. They were poets, he said warily, who felt that love and hate were always worth dying for. They might be Taliban, but if they were, they were hiding it, and they hated all foreigners. Whoever they were, we should not underestimate them, said Genghis; they were armed and they were dangerous.

I held my breath, as he walked in first. Tariq went next, and I crept in behind them. I was getting used to it by now.

The old building felt desolate, its angles and slopes making dark shapes of mystery. The outer room was deserted, except for a pile of rifles stacked in one corner, some with plastic flowers tied to the barrels. They were best quality, brand new and made in Iran, said Genghis, who was an expert on such matters.

The inner chamber was warmed by a fire, glowing at its centre. A Russian samovar was burbling at one end. By the flickering light we felt eyes turning on us like the Eye of Sauron, the faces strong and bearded, some with noses that seemed to have been broken and badly rearranged. Though they could not see my fear, I was sure they could smell it. One, black-turbaned and wild-looking, dredged his lungs and spat on the ground. 'Who is that?' asked the man, pointing towards me.

'No one,' replied Tariq nonchalantly.

'My wife,' lied Genghis, who had remembered Tariq using the same excuse when we were staying at Dostum's. I crept into the corner and sat down, and the action, mercifully, had the effect of diverting the gaze of the man to the flames. He grunted dismissively, and his companions grunted as if echoing him. A general murmur ensued and the staring at the fire resumed.

Behind the others a more menacing shadow was lurking, a tall, gaunt figure wrapped in a blanket, the scarf flapping across his lower face and drawing attention to his sharp eyes. The man told Genghis he was Kaftar's son. He squatted and chatted, hugging his rifle as if he were in love with it. He had won it in battle with the Americans, he said proudly. As I strained to make out his dialect, much of the language evaded me, though the salient bits rang out. By day he fought, by night he studied. In his spare time he dabbled in computers to spread the word, setting up internet sites about *jihad*. He took advantage of the freedom of speech provided by a government powerless to stop them. Many were fed up with not being free to walk, speak, work or talk freely in their own land, and he had joined the cause because of the *kafir* occupation. They were protecting the people from depravity, and fighting for morality and grace. The group nodded in agreement.

'Well, you have your views,' ventured Tariq bravely.

'And they are the true ones,' replied the soldier.

After a short pause and a throat-clearing, Genghis moved on swiftly. 'We believe you are holding a friend of ours,' he growled.

'We may be,' answered the soldier, as silence fell about the room.

'How much do you want?'

'Fifty thousand.'

'Fifty thousand?' cried Tariq.

'One thousand,' boomed Genghis, who was immediately greeted by a bout of spitting and snorts of laughter.

'Five thousand,' offered Genghis.

'Time wasters,' muttered the soldier. 'He would fetch a higher price at market.'

'Five thousand dollars,' said Genghis again, more forcefully this time.

'It is not a good number.'

'It is a good number.'

'Then we will kill him.'

'You would not,' said Tariq, his emotion welling.

'I insist that we speak to Kaftar personally,' ventured Genghis calmly but firmly.

'Kaftar does not fly,' scoffed the soldier.

'We do,' said Genghis, half-smiling.

'Then you must go yourself to Baghlan.'

Genghis was speaking in a dialect that I was glad not to understand. He was already raising himself and signalling to me to follow. I shuffled behind, half shrinking in the doorway, mouth drying, the skin on my arms prickling, my hands shaking so they could hardly have grasped the penknife ready and waiting in my pockets.

As we reached the doorway a voice came from behind. Was my game finally up? By some miracle, not yet it seemed. As we made our way outside I tripped and went flying, catching my breath as an object half-buried in the mud stared back at me. Tariq helped me to my feet, and only afterwards did I work out the broken frame, the torn shreds of material, crushed underfoot by some unknown boot, a dead kite.

We got into the jeep and drove, our chatter dwindling. Now I had finally seen them, those men who held views that had so terrified me, but this time it was not theory, it was real. I returned to my room feeling scared. I was in too deep and there was no going back on things. As I slumped into bed, night weighed on me more heavily than ever, the prospect of light remote.

CHAPTER 22

'When the Tiger Kills, the Jackal Profits'

شکار شیرو خوراک شغال

Maryam burst into the room, as if Karzai had been shot, waggling a paper at us.

'Is it good news, or bad?' asked her brother impatiently.

'I don't know,' she said, passing it to me.

'How much?' Genghis was twitching his whiskers again.

I skimmed it quickly. It was an email from my bank manager. 'Not enough,' I said faintly. The savings I had held at home had all been cashed in, but the sum that had been demanded by Kaftar's son was much higher than we had expected, and it was much more than I had to hand. $50,000! If I counted the overdraft, I had $30,000, and even then we were still $20,000 short.

Tariq looked baffled. 'But you can afford anything!' he cried. 'All foreigners can.'

'No, Tariq,' I said solemnly, 'you are mistaken.'

Shoulders crumpled and heads lowered. Tariq's tone was consolatory. No one would blame me if I went home now.

'No,' I said, but I was still not thinking straight. Not to be outdone, I had an idea that I could borrow the rest, but

I would need to make a phone call. I realised it was madness, but I felt I had to try. They were counting on me.

'That might not be necessary,' said Genghis, who had had his own ideas. 'I think we should go talk to them.'

'But there isn't enough money!' Sohaila was frowning.

'I'm sure we can negotiate,' said Tariq. 'There are always options. They are mountain people, and are not without honour.'

'If they were honourable, they wouldn't have taken him,' said Maryam, dabbing her eyes with her *shalwar khemeez*. It was a very fair point.

'You do not want to give it a try, then?' said Genghis, peering at me, 'It's not too far and you have done it before. You would need to get your outfit straight, of course,' he said camply. Some stretches would require my usual burka disguise, but on others the burka would probably not work. There would be some trekking involved, so I would need good walking boots and warm winter clothing since temperatures in the mountains could drop way below zero. When it came to the risk of altitude sickness, they didn't have a cure, so they would say extra prayers at mosque for me instead.

'It's a very risky journey,' said Tariq, exchanging looks with Sohaila, who was frowning more fiercely than ever.

'You know what she's like,' she groaned.

It was a wise old man who once said, 'One part brave, three parts fool.' Two days later, I had finished the begging and pleading with my bank manager and $30,000 had been wired to Tariq's account in Kabul. We decided to take half in blank traveller's cheques, and half in dollar bills. It wasn't enough, but it was a lot of money, and it was the most I could afford without selling something. After all, I told the others, it was just money. It was people who mattered in life. The Afghans stared at me like an alien. They weren't so sure about that one.

There were so many of us going to see Kaftar that we were driving in two cars, in convoy: the men, the nephews, and four extra heavies who turned out to be police friends of Genghis's. Ahmed, much to everyone's surprise, had been keen to appoint himself to the team, but, fearful that there were already too many people risking themselves, Tariq managed to talk him out of it, on the basis that we needed him in Kabul as a 'control'. Much to Sohaila's protestations, Maryam insisted on joining the party, and when her mother had for the dozenth time failed to talk either of us out of it, she finally relented. Sohaila herself would stay behind to look after the children and the dogs. The importance of the role was not to be underestimated: Little Wolf's cubs were due at any time.

★ ☽ ★

It was just before dawn. The usual bustle of the street had yet to begin, and there was a profound hush upon the old building and the smile of a crescent moon in the sky.

I tried on my mountain outfit. In a feast of layers, I looked like a Michelin woman: hair stuffed beneath hat, trousers too long borrowed from Tariq, rolled at the ends, boots too big, borrowed from Maryam, padded with several woolly socks, giveaway lumps in the chest area smoothed with layers of a strange sack-like material, a large cotton scarf around my neck to hide the face, not to mention the wads of money, stuffed wherever I could hide them. With orange fake tan developing conspicuously on my cheeks, a thick black line around my eyes to ward off the evil eye, even the dog was scared of me. She rolled over and gazed at me, and I kissed the top of her soft head, rubbed the swollen belly and tickled it. It wouldn't be long now.

The convoy was waiting on the corner of the street, two jeeps loaded to bursting point. It was a good job we weren't taking the sidecar. Maryam was wearing her burka, and I mine, and the men had their usual fashion accessories: the guns. Genghis and Tariq smiled wryly when they saw me. That burka positively suited me, they said. I couldn't help taking it as a compliment.

The same great chasms broke the surface of the road, wrecked by war like all the others. As a group of armed soldiers loomed into view, flagged us down, and asked to see our papers, I barely winced in the glare of their scrutiny. Tariq fished out the usual bundle of notes from beneath the dashboard, and after the expected delay and the usual impenetrable exchange in Dari, we moved on. The last time I was here I had seen yellow. Now I saw whiteness. The river had frozen. Where there had been rapids, I saw cascades of ice, suspended as if in enchantment.

As the road began climbing I lifted my visor to a forgotten winter wonderland. Hamlets clung to slopes like limpets, their mud huts seeming to grow out of the rock itself, their footpaths sketching fine lines over crystalline ridges. Snow had been falling, transforming the river into a white road. There were hidden lakes here, said Genghis, but this was no time to search for them.

The day changed as it wore itself out. A mist fell over

the peaks and the temperature dropped to a paralysing cold. The road twisted several times, becoming much steeper, and then suddenly an opening revealed a glacial lake shimmering in the moonlight, at once magical and daunting.

The stardust quickly faded, as the mouth of a tunnel yawned wide into the mountains. The Salang Pass was gloomy, dark, and unforgiving, a place of aggression, hate, and corruption. It was also a minefield, literally, as Tariq pointed out. Armoured trucks crawled at a snail's pace. Great patches of ice and sometimes snow lay thick on the torn asphalt, hiding its perils. Someone had scrawled a message on the rock: 'Be Happy!'. We cheered as we read it and dreamt only of summer.

Beyond the tunnel, ruined buildings lay roofless. They were road workers' huts, said Tariq. They would finish one section, then take their roofs with them to the next stretch. Gradually the snow melted and the road became clearer. Tall pleats of lavender rock stood like vertical blades. There were flashes of movement – donkeys burdened with lumpy sacks and crates, men with ancient, chiselled faces, some with daggers at their sides, or guns. Horses with bells pulled carts, creeping slowly along. Wild sheep grazed on promontories.

At the roadside, stalls sold trout from the mountain rivers. This was Firishtakhan, where it was said the fairies bathed, where the Mujahedin fought against the Russians, the Northern Alliance defeated the Taliban, and mercenaries battled against bandits. It was where Darius, the Persian emperor, had marched, where Babur had driven his army to found the Mughal empire, and Alexander the Great had led his troops – a land overshadowed by ghosts and by history,

A hut lay at the end of a track. Maryam and I looked at each other, hearts plummeting as we realised this was where we were spending the night. There was no heating, of course, so I was glad of my layers. Of the two rooms, one was a cupboard with a bed made for a Lilliputian, with no mattress, and the other was annexed to a bare chamber from which issued an unspeakable stench. Closer inspection revealed the usual hole in the floor over a bottomless pit.

The men lined up their rugs on the floor like sardines in a tin and the door was shut. Maryam and I squeezed into the back room with a tower of filthy blankets and tried rolling out our sleeping bags. We could just lie down, but if we bent our legs we could not turn over. 'It could be worse,' she said, looking on the bright side. We were so exhausted that she proved right. The candle was extinguished, and soon the throat-clearing, coughs and grunts from the other room died down.

Soon I was dreaming. Glimpses of figures with beatific smiles flickered, before the smiles turned sour and the angels turned to judge me. When I woke my fear was real and intense, the wanderings of my imagination wild. A feeling of despair crept up. They felt close now, bolder than ever, those gathering beasts that seemed to smell my fear and draw upon it.

The beasts were not the only problem. My bladder was absolutely bursting. Clasping penknife in one hand and tissue in the other, I opened the door, which squeaked loudly, dancing on tiptoe over the snoring bodies. I went out into the open where it was so cold I couldn't feel my fingers as they fumbled around the layers. What was worse was that other places where it really counted were numb too. I breathed and squatted, as about a hundred yards away something flashed against the rock. I shied back, uncertain if it were beast or man. I looked on the ground and saw there were two trails of shapeless imprints, one foot-sized and the other paw-sized, converging and separating again. I wondered what they could be, and in my haste to get back inside slipped on the frozen ground, almost stabbing myself with the penknife. A distant howl echoed around the pass, the cry of a she-wolf. I returned to the hut in despair. I wondered if I would ever see my family again.

Some of the others were already up and moving. Snow was being melted on a small gas stove someone had brought, tea steamed over metal cups, and the tiny room was filled with the scent of rosewater from Genghis's aftershave. Maryam looked at me with a strength that gave me courage. Her brother put his arm reassuringly around her shoulder. These people were Pashtun, he said, like they were. Blood was not their only currency, and neither was revenge. There would be honour too; it was the old tribal order.

He delved into his pocket, fished out something and handed it to me. As I saw the jewel-like pages, the beautiful script, I could hardly believe it. It was Ismael's Qur'an. 'Where did you get that?' I cried.

'We knew you wouldn't take it,' he said sheepishly, 'but Ismael wanted you to have it. You can trade it.'

I glanced at him crossly, but had to admit it awarded me courage. 'Allah is indeed with us,' I said, and he smiled. I gathered up the money and handed it to Genghis.

'Are you ready?' he said, wrapping it gently in a soft green cloth to protect it.

'Yes,' I said.

'*Khoob*, good,' he boomed as we climbed into the jeep, '*Imrooz dastaane ma khoon aalood ast*, today we wear blood on our hands!' It was an old Afghan expression that meant we put ourselves in danger.

In truth I was as ready as I ever would be. I knew exactly what I was doing. I still hadn't forgiven myself yet for the day in Tavistock Square, when I had been powerless to make a difference at the scene of the bus bombing. I wasn't afraid to die. More than ever, I felt that I deserved to.

★ ☽ ★

Beyond the mountains the sunrise was luminous. A waterfall was cascading against the rock, in its mist a rainbow. Around it the early light broke through in patches. There were Arctic foxes here, said Tariq, as if to take our mind off things, marmots and wolves, wagtails and hoopoes and eagles, even. There were larks, too, said to sing so hard and fly so high they became dizzy and fell to the earth. If a dog ate one, it would go mad, he said.

The road twisted downwards, between slabs and boulders, the track crumbling at the edges into sheer drops above a valley stubbled with hawthorn. Above us a huge bird was circling. Genghis thought it was a vulture, but I think he said that to wind me up.

It was several hours before Genghis signalled, and a debate followed among the men in language I did not understand. It was not far, said Tariq at last. We would tackle the rest by foot, but we must stick to the pathway and stay close behind Genghis. Mines were everywhere, and that was apart from the 'simple ambushes' and 'spontaneous muggings' that were frequent in these parts.

While the men loaded the rucksacks, Maryam and I decided to abandon our burkas. It was a high-risk strategy, but, all things considered, it was important that we could see where we were treading, or we might fall. As we made our way slowly, stumbling in the grip of vertigo, fear saturated me. I felt helpless and pathetic. The radios had stopped working and there was no mobile reception. I reached out in my thoughts to those closest to me, hoping they would forgive me for my recklessness, as gradually the urge to scream subsided.

The valley of Darisujan looked golden in the rising mist, as if everything was in harmony. Burkas rode side-saddle. Small children struggled with sacks on their backs. Armed men strained at bridles, coaxing their stallions with whistles and flicks of the whip. Goats climbed over the rocks, and below, where the land sloped down there were a few walled-in rice terraces. Shaggy camels bore strangely shaped loads along the roadside. I wondered what their cargoes were. The men said they thought opium and weapons were openly for sale here. In the distance I spotted pick-up trucks carrying people and more weapons. Where were they heading? Over the border to Pakistan, or back from it? Were they Taliban? They didn't appear to be, but then who was I to tell? Genghis said they were smugglers.

A sound began echoing around the mountainside. It waned and returned, lifted, and carried, wailing, down the valley. We stopped in our tracks and listened. *'Allahu Akbar, Allahu Akbar . . .'* The song ebbed, and was replaced by a familiar chanting. Maryam took my hand and squeezed it.

God was with us, she said; it was the sound of men praying.

We continued along the rocky path, and soon the mouth of a cave yawned in the rock face. We craned our necks and Tariq borrowed my binoculars. It was only then we saw the rough and feral-looking men properly. Some of them were poachers, thought Genghis. He could tell by their guns. Deep in prayer, they stood in rows, raising their hands to their shoulders, right hands over their left on their chests, using words alien to me but made meaningful by their emotion. They prayed silently for a few moments, then repeated the whole motion of lying down, finally sighing and wiping their faces. We paused a while, and the men with me laid down their arms and mouthed the words in imitation. I silently said my own prayer, for my father's life.

Maryam and I dug into our rucksacks and slipped on our burkas again. It would be safer that way, said Genghis, and the path was less treacherous from here on so we would be less likely to trip and fall off the mountain. He was right. The slope became wider, and seemed less steep. Through the net of my burka I made out a few mud structures. I lifted my visor to get a better look. Piles of ammunition lay openly on the ground. Bandoliers of bullets dangled like Chinese lanterns, and there were crates of rifles, and sacks. I assumed they held opium.

A few hundred yards away lay a fortified building. Outside it a figure was standing, hunched, thickset, and cloaked in grey. It turned, and I caught a better view of it, of the ruddy face and small, proud eyes. There a bitterness about it, as if it had no interest in us. I looked again and blinked, for the figure I saw was not a man, but a woman. Her name was Bibi Ayesha, well known in these parts as Kaftar. She was Afghanistan's only female warlord.

Genghis and Tariq walked ahead, while Maryam and I hung back. I was glad they had gone first, since in any case I dared not move, and I was frozen to the spot with fear. A lizard slipped over my shoe as if to enquire the purpose of our visit, then jumped off. Should we go back to the jeep? It was an unrealistic option. Too many people had seen us now. There was a torrent of Pashto, a nod of heads, and Tariq was beckoning us to follow. Heads lowered, concealed by our burkas, we obeyed him.

In a bare mud room men sat on the ground that was just brown dust. One of the men we recognised: Kaftar's son. Kaftar herself sat like an ancient ruin, clasping the Russian Makarov pistol she kept close to her heart in a shoulder holster. We crept in at the back, and listened. The men were talking agitatedly, Genghis holding out a bit of the money and waving it. Kaftar shot him a look, raw and hard, before summoning her guards. In the commotion a man fell to the ground, bound and blindfolded, hands tied behind his back, struggling to breathe under his gag. Tariq rushed over, observing with consternation the figure, which was thin as a reed, with torn clothes. Was it Zaki? Through the mesh of the burka I couldn't make him out properly. At our safe distance we still felt unsafe, but Maryam bravely risked whispering a translation of the Pashto so I could understand.

'We shall see if you are liars like Karzai,' scowled Kaftar, taking the money, and then throwing it back again.

'It is enough!' barked Genghis in his great, deep voice.

'It is not!' snapped Kaftar. glancing around suspiciously, and then pausing for a moment, as if suddenly distracted by something, her eye resting on the book peeking out from the top of Tariq's jacket. 'What is that?' she croaked.

'It is just a book,' said Tariq, but Kaftar was shouting again, narrowing her eyes and flaring her nostrils.

'Give it to me,' she ordered. Tariq delved into his pocket, unwrapped the book and handed it to her. Leafing through the pages, she seemed unimpressed. She tossed it to her son, who glanced at it momentarily and hurled it back again. Tariq picked it up and covered it gently with the green cloth. Trading it was useless, it seemed. The Kaftar did not read.

Genghis was fiddling with his phone and dialling. It looked as if he was up to something, though I couldn't make out what. 'Stop!' he boomed suddenly, and then everything stood still as he passed the handset to Kaftar. We waited silently as a conversation unfolded, and although the words went over my head there was no misunderstanding the look of blind fury on Kaftar's ragged face. 'An eye for an eye, blood for blood!' she muttered. She motioned to her men, the man was unbound, and through the bars of my visor, suddenly I caught sight of him. The man on the ground was Zaki.

★ ☽ ★

Shots rang out in the air as we made our way, stumbling, back to the vehicles. Zaki was so weak he could hardly walk, so Tariq supported him. The engine jerked with a flustered scuffle of springs and though Tariq tapped his hand at the wheel, it would go no faster. The dust evaporated, and Maryam's face emerged, smudged with tears. Zaki glanced at her, his own face distant, haunted. Their eyes brushed and they looked away quickly.

As we rocked down the track, Genghis lifted his head to the sky and smiled.

'What did you give her?' I gasped.

'A message from the one man she feared,' he grinned. As I glanced at him questioningly, I knew there was no need to fear. That man, I had no doubt, was General Dostum. Tribal allegencies ran deep. Zaki was Uzbek and so was Dostum. Dostum had saved him, and it hadn't cost me a penny.

PART THREE

Sore Feet

CHAPTER 23

'There is Always a Path
to the Top of the Highest Mountain'

کوه هر قدر بلند باشد باز هم بالا خود راه دارد

Zaki lay in the back seat and said hardly a word, though the bruises on his legs were eloquent. His head sat huge upon his body, limbs frail as if they might snap. In the small movements of his features, the brow lifted or lowered, the eyes narrowed or widened, we watched the story spinning out inside him. It was a face that seemed almost painful to look at – withdrawn, sunken, all animation gone. At last he seemed to find a little peace, once clenching his fists and leaning forward, then collapsing back again.

As he slept, Maryam sketched patterns with her fingers on the window. His secret griefs could wait. One day he would let her in to the darkness, but it was not this day.

At last we were back. A light frost wrapped the city in icy petals. Twilight was falling, and a few solitary lamps were twinkling. In Kharabat, the old musician's quarter, a reedy melody wafted on the air, as if everything had become beautiful again.

I waved the others goodbye, and wiggled the great yellow key left helpfully in the lock by Sohaila. The stale smell had ebbed, and the comforting scent of baking *naan* permeated the stairwell. A few paw prints wove patterns in the dust, but the dog herself was nowhere to be seen and the food bowl was empty. I lay on the bed and tried to summon the energy to search for her, but my limbs ached with exhaustion. Almost immediately my eyelids shut, and I blanked out.

It must have been hours before I opened them again. Ten centimetres from my face two anxious buttons of eyes looked back, wide open and gleaming in the half-light. And there she was, scruffy tail, shabby ears, long bony legs, head resting on her front paws. I threw my arms around her neck and buried my nose in the fur. 'Little Wolf,' I said softly, and as the tail wagged and the head lifted, it made my soul sing.

That night my mind refused to stop turning. I tried desperately to unravel how and why Dostum had let Zaki off, and what Genghis had said to facilitate the situation. Was it just about the tribal connection? That seemed too easy. Genghis said the information was sacred, and not to be passed on. It was enough for me to know that Dostum had honour and, in her own way, so did Kaftar. It seemed hard to believe: she was, after all, a kidnapper.

But I was wrong, I found out later. The Kaftar, Genghis insisted, represented an intriguing alternative model of Afghan womanhood, one that was much older than the Mujahedin, the Communists, or even the Taliban. She was part of an ancient tradition of women who took up arms to outshine their men in bravery, however brutal the consequences. Early Afghan historical works had been littered with such women. I had even studied them; I just never expected to meet one. There was Shah Bori, said to have lived the life of a warrior and who died fighting the troops of Emperor Babur in the 16th century. Two centuries later, Nazoana had reputedly protected the fortress of Zabul with her sword, and just a hundred years after that, Malalay of Maiwand had led a successful rebellion against the British, using her headscarf as a banner.

Only now did all the jigsaw pieces surrounding the kidnap begin to fall into place. Though he had no proof, Tariq believed that Dostum had always secretly known where Zaki was being held and why, and that it was not just about the money. There was a deeper level, of which Genghis had been aware and had tried to protect us from knowing, for our own safety. Zaki had been a suspected informant to the Allied Forces, and a pawn in a game that was useful to both sides of the conflict in the south. When Dostum's aide had sent us to Herat, he was aware of the potential advantages to their own position in the matter, but knew it might take time for any useful information to emerge. They had simply been buying time.

As it turned out, Zaki admitted nothing when he was interrogated on the subject, so that in the end it was decided he knew nothing or, at least, that there was nothing new in what he told his captors. When Dostum found out that it was an innocent life at risk, he had personally intervened, at Genghis's request, to secure Zaki's release. Honour was at stake, all right, and there were allegiances, but there was more to it even than that. Genghis had warned Dostum that, if he did not intervene, I would be sure to tell the British government that he had abandoned a man who might have been a great help to them. Dostum's own position might have been compromised for holding back information that would be useful in the fight against the Taliban. Of course, we could prove none of it.

According to Tariq it was not man who had spared us anyway. Ismael's holy book had protected us. We had been saved by the word of God.

★ ☽ ★

In the days that followed, Zaki was in decompression mode, as, in a sense, we all were. New clothes of cool cotton made him feel strange, rather than human again. He could not eat much, his stomach still unaccustomed to meat. He revelled in the light of the sky that had so long been denied him. He did not want to sleep, he wanted to walk, faster and faster, until he was running. The feel of sun on his skin was dazzling after so long in the gloom. But still the pain lingered in his eyes, as if he were reaching out for something he could not quite grasp. It was the look I had seen in the eyes of the prisoner in Makroyan.

Unable to bear the dark, Zaki slept with the light on. The scuttling of mice reminded him of the creatures who had shared his captivity, and his nightmares haunted him desperately. At the medical centre, the doctors treated his wounds, but nothing could heal the invisible scars of his imprisonment. Memories he wanted to forget burst out unexpectedly – the cramped conditions, the hiss from the radio that goaded him night and day, the oil lamp that gave out an intermittent flicker of light and heat.

At my insistence, Tariq had promised to return Ismael's Qur'an to him. It was a lucky Qur'an, he said. After all, it was the Qur'an. Genghis and his nephews returned to the fields to tend their sheep, and I lay low for a few days. I called home as often as the phone lines would allow, brimming with the news of Zaki's release and discussing my plans to return. The weather was beautiful, I told my mother. I kept quiet about the guns, the mines, the narrow escapes which would only have given her a heart attack. I was grateful to hear her voice, and to learn that my father's health appeared to be improving. He was home again, said my mother ecstatically, albeit surrounded by medical paraphernalia and with more medicines than you were likely to find in the whole of Kabul. He was reading poetry, as there were fewer words and he could think about them more. He still liked to talk about food, though he was being fed through a tube.

Every day, Zaki's strength was returning, but finding his way back from the terrible conditions imposed on him was going to take time. With his health in mind, it was agreed not to rush things where the wedding was concerned. There was plenty of time. He had to find his feet again, and learn how to live normally. We all realised the healing process would take a long time, however strong a man he was, and so the adjustment to a different reality began gently. As he began to laugh again, it seemed to me his laughter gave hope for the human spirit. We were all in awe of him, but most of all Maryam. She and the wedding were to Zaki a signpost, a light by which he could see the way. The prospect of their life together gave him hope.

For now the fact of his being alive was enough cause for celebration. We had made it. Mr Omar couldn't agree more, he said, and his advice was unequivocal. We were lucky to have made it. You never knew what life would throw at you, so you should never take chances. It was always better to be on the safe side. 'Before you criticise someone, walk for a mile in their shoes,' he said. 'Then you'll be a mile away and have their shoes. . .'

'*Man een ra ba yaad khod negah midaaram,*' I promised him. It meant that I would bear it in mind.

★ ☽ ★

At the bakery, Little Wolf had disappeared yet again. She was not in the yard, and her food bowl was untouched. I threw up my arms in dismay. Then, suddenly, there came a whimper. I got down on my hands and knees, and two round pools gleamed out from the darkness beneath the bed. She was nesting.

After I had collected myself I began heating the stove, and left an emergency message for Tariq and Maryam to bring clean towels and alcohol, purely for antiseptic purposes of course. Meanwhile I smothered my hands in alcohol gel, and boiled some water. I had read about it somewhere, but that was for babies, and I wasn't sure if it was the same for puppies. I was winging it. It felt like an age before Maryam and Tariq appeared at the door, in such a flurry that clouds of dust swirled from fissures in the wall.

The night wore on in silence. A whimper or two, then nothing. I stroked the head and tried to reassure her. By 2 a.m. she was straining again. If we watched closely we could actually see her belly moving with the contractions. At 3 a.m. the first pup arrived, pale, just like his mother. We wiped away the slippery covering, rubbed the little back, and doused the umbilical cord with the vodka that Tariq had brought. Drinking was a sin, but alcohol as medicine was a godsend. Little Wolf was too weak to bite, so I cut the cord with my nail scissors, any sense of euphoria quickly lost in the panic of trying to get it right. Maryam placed the pup next to a teat, and immediately he attached himself to it.

Half an hour later, Little Wolf strained again. This time there were two puppies, followed by two placentas. Then came another, but this one, unlike the others, showed flesh through the thin hair that was a sickly yellow rather than pink. Its tail lay still, and the perfectly formed little legs lay limply. I massaged its back more firmly, but it still did not move, so I blew in its mouth, which was an odd feeling. I tousled it in the towel again. Suddenly there was a hint of pink around the nose, a twitch, then all its body flushed beneath the downy hair, and its mouth opened. It was alive! Tariq put it close beside a teat and there it stayed feeding until the next and last puppy arrived, which came out tail first. We mixed an egg with milk and crushed in some vitamin tablets, but with a bundle of furry blind balls at her stomach, Little Wolf, too exhausted to drink, dropped off immediately. As I watched them snuggling, everything felt perfect.

'Shall we?' I asked, vodka bottle in one hand, kettle in the other.

They glared at me hard and held up their tea glasses.

'To freedom!'

'We'll all drink to that!' said Tariq,

'And what will you toast?' Maryam asked him.

'Peace . . .' said her brother, clinking his tea glass against my vodka. 'And what will you toast, sister?'

'Friendship,' said Maryam, having thought for a moment, at which we clinked our glasses as one.

It was almost light by the time they left. After they had gone, I put another stick of wood on the fire and watched the flickering gleams it cast on the greasy walls. As the flames danced it was impossible not to feel comforted by their warmth. In the darkness I could hear the pups whimpering faintly, as I buried my head among cushions that muffled my tears. At last they were tears of joy.

CHAPTER 24

'The Sun Cannot be Hidden with Two Fingers'

آفتاب به دو انگشت پنهان کنی نمی‌شود

I opened my eyes with a mixture of emotions, soothed by the sight of a hairy, moist nose and a bundle of tiny bodies. Nature had kicked in, and I felt all I could do was to let it take its course – which was lucky, because vets here were rare as snow leopards. I glanced at my watch and fell asleep again, hardly noticing the din outside.

Ten past ten, and the pups were still sleeping. I studied them and checked their breathing, surprised that they looked so pink and healthy. Even the little one that I had revived looked perky. I rearranged their blanket and they wriggled slightly but didn't whimper. Only a knock at the door brought a faint noise from their direction, and it was not just the door that squeaked as I opened it slowly. Tariq's pale face softened as he glimpsed them. He had come to check I was all right, he sighed, but he wasn't fooling anyone.

He also brought news. Zaki had slept well, and now it appeared he wanted to talk about his experience, and he wanted me to be there so that I could tell people in my country. Part of me dreaded to hear what he might have to say, but later that day we gathered together in the front room of the house. With the pups doing well, I had wondered about leaving them. Pup-sitting services were hastily engaged as Sohaila volunteered to keep an eye on them, and Omar drove me to Deh Mazang.

At the house the men were deep in conversation, Genghis puffing smoke rings, Tariq stroking his stubbly chin. Only the women were absent: the men wouldn't want to alarm them by anything that was said, but as a foreign woman I was used to such things. I took it as a compliment. Zaki's accent was strong, so Tariq translated. We talked for a while about our countries, before Zaki lit a match and began his story. As it all poured out of him I sat silently and listened.

The day he had been taken had been like any other, he said. He had just been crossing the road by the Charahe de Mazang, thinking how good life was, when it had happened. As he hurried along towards Asmai Wat he hardly registered the masked face shouting at him to get down or else he would shoot. Another masked man took his watch, his phone, the few *afghanis* he had in his pocket, and his shoes. The shoes he regretted most, they were his dignity. He was bundled into the car, his wrists and ankles pressed together and bound. In the commotion that followed a cloth was put over his head so tightly he could hardly breathe.

When he woke up, his head was splitting. He could reach out and touch the wall, then shuffle to and fro, contained by the chains around his legs. When night fell the darkness seemed only to intensify the heat. Noises took on gigantic proportions in his imagination, the buzz of insects as loud as if they were inside his head. He lay sweating, panting, his mind racing, surrounded by cockroaches, crawling and scratching monsters. Sleep brought no peace. The *jinn* were everywhere, he said, those creatures invisible to human eye but which were said to be made of fire. There were good and bad *jinn*. The good inspired prophets, soothsayers and poets; the evil, the *shaytan*, preyed on the faithful.

At last dawn came. By the filtered light cast by a grille in the ceiling he saw the walls of the cell, the smooth monotony of the mud, the limits of the space. A key rattled in the lock. Muffled voices came close. Who were they? Someone came in, put down some water and left. That first day dragged more interminably than any other, he said. He spent the time trying to work out where he was and who was holding him, trying to ignore the stench of the place, scratching the bites and lumps on his body, battle scars of the night.

The faces of the guards were covered, so that he could hardly tell them apart. Visits from the guards gave an idea of the time, though without his watch he had no real sense of it. He was fed like a dog in a cage, he said. The guard would bring a candle as he brought food; then he would leave him. In the silence he could hear mumblings from the room next door, but though he would strain his ears, he could make no words out. Through the grille he would try to figure out the position of the sun, so he could perform his prayers. During those first hours he began planning his escape, thinking through how he would overcome his captors. Realistically he knew any such attempt was futile, but the thought kept him going, anyway. In the heat of the day, he dozed to kill time, still buoyed up with hope that he would soon be released. He had done nothing wrong, had he?

How little a man knows about himself until he is locked away on his own, Zaki said, lighting up a Pine Light cigarette. Through a split in the wall he could just make out shapes, but it was the fissures in his thoughts and emotions that cast the spotlight on to the darkest places – his fears, his weaknesses. Being confined in this way, he was forced to leave the past behind and live entirely in the moment. In captivity, the mind unfolds by itself. In the darkness, his imagination ran riot, so powerful that at times he cried out in frustration, his emotions veering wildly between hope, despair, anger and acceptance.

The nights in that airless cell were the worst. The filtered light cast by the grille disappeared and he was left with nothing but thick blackness, a darkness in which he could not rest. As the hours and days dragged on, the future stretched ahead, as murky as the walls and as inscrutable. To while away the time he would try to focus on all that was good about his life, so that he felt grateful – blessed, even – and the intensity of thought and feeling brought an exhaustion such as he had never experienced.

He would retreat to lost paradises of his childhood memory, watching the soldiers as a boy, copying their poses, having fierce kite fights with his friends. He would dream of food – sizzling kebabs and onions, *palau, qorma* and *sheer yakh*, ice-cream, in the baking heat. Dishes his mother used to make rose so vividly now in his imagination that he swore he could smell the hot *naan* baking in the *tandoor*. As children they had been poor.

They would huddle together for warmth in the cold winters with only *homach,* flour soup, to warm them. It was not really the food, but being together, that had been important. Now he scrabbled to remember their games – playing *barfi* with his friends; putting fresh new snow into an envelope and leaving it teasingly in his grandmother's kitchen, then running away giggling before she noticed; dreaming of the feast she would cook for them.

Often he would recite poetry to himself, straining to remember the exact words and verses: Baydel the Mongol poet, Sana'i the court poet of the Ghaznavids, Baba the mystic, and Jami the wise man of Herat. Jami had spent eighteen years alone in the mountains near Jam, studying the Qur'an and the religious sciences. He chose isolation and triumphed over it. As the poems came back to Zaki, fragments at first, then lines and sometimes whole verses, he spoke them aloud, his audience of mice, rats and insects scurrying around regardless of his oratory. 'Don't be blurry-eyed, See me clearly, See my beauty without the old eyes of delusion.'

He found solace in the words of his hero, the great Jalaluddin Rumi: 'You mustn't be afraid of death, You are a deathless soul, You can't be kept in a dark grave, You are filled with God's glow.' 'Why cling to life?' Rumi had said. 'The sun dies and dies squandering a hundred lives lived every instant.' Death, after all, was our wedding with eternity. It was when our soul would take wings and soar with the angels. Though he could not imagine what that meant exactly, Zaki contented himself with the thought. The words of Rumi filled him with strength. They spoke of freedom, of the strength of the human spirit to suffer and overcome. Above all, they spoke of love.

In the darkness his thoughts dwelled on his marriage to Maryam. From the moment he saw her photograph he knew she was the one for him. She was the most beautiful girl he had ever seen – nice round figure, full behind, good nose. The nose was important. When it came to bearing his children, it would be a good thing they had Maryam's genes to inherit, his own nose being so huge, like a potato. For a husband to admire the beauty of his wife was to honour Allah, who created her. Her loveliness, like her love, was reserved for him and guarded from the eyes of other men by the veil. The beauty of a woman was an example of God's creation, and soon Maryam's would be his alone.

As he thought of her he felt a profound sense of longing. He wanted to know her deeply and to share his life with her. It was at this moment, he thought, that he first felt true love for her. Or perhaps it was just the idea of loving her that intoxicated him. Whatever that feeling was, it rushed through his body in a great wave of excitement.

Sometimes he would be blindfolded, the guards whistling happily as they left him alone again to say their prayers. Then there were the beatings, apparently for no reason. Occasionally a guard would remove his blindfold as if to check he was still breathing. Sometimes there would be coffee and even a cigarette, then another beating. The first time he had been beaten he had waited for it with dread. He knew they would beat him and lie to him, use tactics to frighten him. You never saw the punch coming, or where on your body the blow would land.

The first time it happened he saw a light blazing through his blindfold. He sat in silence, half-naked, hands tied behind his back, steeling himself. The guard burst in and began speaking. 'What is your name? Where do you live?' At first the voice was calming, the questions matter-of-fact. But then the guard leaned forward. 'What have you told the enemy?' he asked, calmly and softly again and again.

'I told them the Taliban would never give up,' Zaki said. 'They just wanted the occupiers to leave.'

The guard treated him like an infidel, quoting from the book they both loved, both read and knew by heart. It was an eye for an eye, a tooth for a tooth, he told Zaki. He deserved to be punished, did he not? The blows started, heavy and deliberate. The butt of the Kalashnikov pounded into him, the blows raining down on his chest, his thighs and legs and then on his tender parts. Knowing that to cry out would only make it worse, he screamed inside, feeling a rage that was so great that at last he no longer felt the pain. He and the guards were brothers of Afghanistan and of Islam, but they were not of the same stuff. The blows kept coming, but still Zaki restrained himself, too proud to shout out.

At last he felt a cigarette being pushed between his lips, and heard the spark of a match and an instruction: 'Smoke.' Zaki obeyed, before something strange happened. There was a commotion, with doors banging and the usual shouting, but this time it was a woman's voice who addressed him, sharp and hard, like rusted metal. Then the same old question, again, again and again. 'What did you tell them?'

'Nothing. I swear,' said Zaki.

'Do you want to die?' the voice sounded cold, uninterested, as the beating began again, this time without mercy.

Afterwards he was shaking and trembling uncontrollably. As he prayed fervently, and squirmed uncomfortably, it seemed to him that anything was better than this confinement. Once or twice he screamed out, begging Allah to set him free, and as he reached with his chained fist to punch the wall he hardly noticed the pain or the blood as it welled between his fingers. Thoughts of those he loved, of Maryam, soothed him. As the rage subsided a great strength began surging through him, his thoughts of death replaced by those of escape from the suffering. To be alive and dwell in the moment was a necessity, for his sanity, for his survival.

After that first time, he bore his inquisitions without fear. The more he refused to buckle, the more he felt his captors' fear. They were his prisoners also, and they would die too, some day, when Allah himself would judge them.

Was he going to be killed? He didn't know, but in any case he was not to fear death, his father had once told him. God determined both the length of an individual's life and also when the universe would cease to exist. Forty days before death, a leaf with the name of the person who was to die fell from the tree beneath the throne of God. From this sign Izrail, the angel of death, would know the appointed time had come. As Zaki remembered this, he wondered if his leaf had already fallen, but the more he thought about it the less he feared death. For the good man it was a time of justice. At the moment it came upon him, a book recording his deeds would be fixed to his neck. If he was destined for heaven, he would be given the book of his life to hold in his right hand. The account of his life would be balanced on the scales of judgement and his destination determined by which side was heavier. It was said that good deeds weighed more than bad ones, but only God himself knew the weight of good necessary to merit access to paradise.

The actual process of separating the soul from the body also depended on the record of good or bad deeds. If the human was a bad person in life, his soul was ripped out painfully, but if he was a righteous person, his soul separated from him like a drop of water falling from glass. There was no purgatory, no halfway house between heaven and hell in which the sins of those not yet ready for heaven could be purged. In death, the body remained in the ground while the soul lay between the two worlds, between death and resurrection. After he had been greeted by the grave, he would attempt a journey through the seven heavens to see what lay ahead, when Munkar and Nakir, two black angels with piercing blue eyes would appear. 'Who is your lord?' they would ask. Only martyrs and prophets skipped the interrogation and went directly to heaven, and Zaki wasn't one of those.

As he pondered his life his deeds weighed heavy on him. He felt guilty for things he had said and done, wondering if it was too late, if now the time to apologise had been snatched from him for ever. Even more he regretted the things that he had not done. The idea of paradise glittered for him, a golden refuge, a state beyond imagination, in which sensory pleasures, and financial, physical and emotional desires were meaningless. Heaven was Allah's reward to us for the losses and sacrifices suffered on this earth; it was a place for happiness, reward and, above all, love.

In the blackness of his cell he would imagine the colours, wild and vibrant, and the scents, an exotic mix of musk, ginger, and amber. He would picture the angels, the trees, the birds and the rivers, and think of the *hoors*, white and pure, like gazelles with faces like crescent moons. They would have translucent flesh and large, appealing black eyes, their bodies made of saffron, musk, amber and camphor, and their hair of raw silk. In paradise there was water, milk and honey, wine that could be drunk without intoxicating, and food to satisfy the grossest appetite.

One night he had been dreaming such thoughts, his mouth watering, when suddenly he heard something. At first he thought he was imagining it, but the longer it continued the more he became convinced that it was real. Tap, tap, tap. The tune was twisting, winding, reaching. He was not imagining it. Someone was playing a *rubab*.

He dragged himself up, and moved his feet forwards, slowly at first, chains clinking in time to the beat, shuffling awkwardly. Then, as he got into the rhythm, he moved faster and more energetically, until at last he was leaping, bumping into the walls with his hands and feet, until sweat was pouring from him. And in this letting go he felt suddenly alive and unafraid – of his captors, of what the future might hold, of everything that had ever daunted him. At last he was so transported that it felt as if he was not dancing alone, but as if there was something else with him there – as if it was with the darkness itself that he was dancing. He was not sure how long he danced in this way, but it felt like a very long time before he collapsed back down, exhausted.

As he sank into a dreamless sleep, he was still reeling from the ecstasy of the dancing. It was as if the pokey little cell was streaming with light. He smelt amber, musk, rose petals, orange blossom, and the flowers of jasmine, geranium, laurel or eglantine, and his heart felt cleansed of all the images that had haunted him. That night he remembered more vividly than all the others, he said. He never heard the music again, but it would sing to him inside, as he lay there, and he would sing back, loud, fearless and out of tune.

As the days and weeks rolled by, his determination grew as his strength declined. How much longer could it go on? No one would be able to afford the ransom, anyway. How could he expect them to? He had already used all his money for the wedding. He wondered now where his body would be found and who would find it. Would it be his elderly parents? Or his brothers? And how would his future bride react? The thought brought a sickness to his empty belly. Better no body, he thought. It would be too much for any of them to bear.

Fortunately, he thought, such reflections would soon be behind him, for his ordeal was about to end. Distant shouts were followed by much commotion, and he thought his time was up. He was ready now, ready for anything. Something struck him, and his legs gave way beneath him. As he opened his eyes and heard someone say his name he could hardly believe it. This time the voice was one he recognised. It was Tariq's.

★ ☽ ★

He paused then, faltering, and only now I noticed his trembling hands. He did not blame his captors, he said. Bad things happened to people going about their daily lives every day, but he was an Afghan. Like their fathers and grandfathers, they were stubborn and strong.

He had learnt many things, things that had broadened and deepened him, that he would never have known so well had he not been imprisoned: patience, forgiveness, above all, balance. His suffering had changed him for ever – his dreams were different now. In a way he was grateful, and most of all he appreciated the darkness, for it was through that darkness that he felt close to God and more loved by him. He felt more alive than he had ever done.

CHAPTER 25

'She Hasn't Time to Scratch her Head'

وقت به سرخاریدن هم ندارد .

It was to be a whirlwind wedding, Afghan style. Negotiations had long since taken place about the *mahr*, the financial amount given by the groom in the case of divorce, and the *jehz*, the dowry. There would be two ceremonies. First came the *nikah*, the signing of contracts, and then came the *arusi*, to which guests were invited. Everything was happening on one day and everything was last-minute. There was just enough time for a super-quick henna night.

The mud-floored room was bare, except for a portrait of Karzai between posters of women with different hairstyles and a few empty display cases. Brushes, bushy and thin, large and tiny, were laid out like surgical instruments. Chairs with worn seats lay beneath the hair-dryers, of the antique single-domed variety, bolted together with wires and pistons. Every seat was taken. Everyone wanted to look their best. Some were having their faces 'smoothed', others were having their hair done, and Sohaila and Maryam were having the full works.

An excitement had taken hold of the women. They could abandon their housework and make themselves beautiful. It had little to do with their husbands, with whom they hardly spent any time at all. They were doing it for Allah, themselves, and each other.

Within the privacy of the salon, the ladies shared their gossip like the air they breathed. The groom was a brave man, a good man, and a rich one, they agreed. His mother was a dragon, but he didn't let that bother him. He had suffered more than most men, and had proved himself to everyone.

'Is he handsome?' asked the hairdresser.

'Yes!' cried the ladies excitedly, nodding and conferring. 'He is gorgeous!'

The hairdresser sighed dreamily. She herself was nuts for the actor Zayed Khan. He was engaged, but she could be his second wife.

Only Maryam was not laughing, her face as white as the bleaching agent the hairdresser was applying. 'I'm worried,' she said shakily, listing her insecurities. Zaki still felt like a stranger to her. How should she talk and act with him now, after all he had been through? Too familiar was not the done thing. Too distant, and it would seem uncaring. Her mother looked non-plussed. It was just the usual round of natural wedding nerves.

The hairdresser took some cotton thread and twisted it into a loop held with her hand and teeth. Slowly and diligently she worked over the face, teasing out the small hairs until the cheeks became pink, 'Would you like me to do yours?' she asked me afterwards, taking a penknife and pinching the eyebrows. 'No thanks,' I said quickly.

Hair was lathered, brushed, combed and curled. Dryers hummed, scissors snipped. False eyelashes fluttered. Lips shone scarlet with Pakistani lipstick that left a chemical aftertaste. In a final flourish the hairdresser swirled her toxic-smelling hairspray. At last the hairdos were ready. Hair done in curlicues no hurricane could dislodge would be able to withstand a force ten gale, but most of all, the burka.

We walked down the street like an old-fashioned angel cake, Maryam in white, her mother in blue, and myself in pink – supermodels, ready to take on a world that would never set eyes on us.

★ ☽ ★

Paper lanterns and coloured bulbs laced the tiny courtyard of the house. The hot air smelt of sweat and lemonade. Jewels twinkled like the eyes of the women. Voices trilled like the chirrup of nightingales. Grandchildren carried henna in wickerwork baskets. Mothers drew dark paste over hands and feet, then wrapped them and tied them. It was time to let our hair down. Sisters, aunts, cousins and nieces shimmied to the beat of Ahmed Zahir, the Elvis of the Middle East.

I had bought two singing birds in cages as a wedding gift and passed them to Maryam. We placed the cages beside each other and the two birds tweeted slightly. Maryam held out her hand to coax them, and one flinched and jumped onto its finger perch, chirruping sweetly. She put the cages on the floor and suddenly they stopped. It seemed the birds sang only when they could see each other.

The twang of a gut string took over. The pitch faltered and subsided into a sequence of notes that seemed to struggle, unresolved, as if aspiring to a conclusion that was destined always to remain out of its grasp. The women turned, as if searching for something. Faces flashed like petals, arms were raised gracefully. Then they froze, flounced, pitching their heads back and straightened. Arms fell on the beat again, bodies twisting, backs arching. Heels rose, insteps arched. Feet drew shapes in the dust before straight necks softened and slumped, fluttering to their knees in exhaustion. It was a dance of togetherness, of purity and grace.

I smiled idiotically and joined in, and the world whirled past. In the heady butterflying there was nothing to stop the memories dancing, of the day in the square that had changed my life, of my father's disease, and my mother's selflessness.

As I left them that evening they handed out roses. Marriage was a blessing, they said, but it was freedom that was the elusive flower.

★ ☽ ★

I woke up having slept straight through the song of the muezzin. There had been a happy phone call from home: everything was fine, my mother had said. My father was recovering. He was looking forward to seeing me soon. It was more than any of us could have hoped for. I dragged myself up, splashed yellow water on my eyes, and brushed my teeth with Chinese toothpaste in yellow water. I even accidentally swallowed some.

In the corner of the room the dogs looked a picture. The little blind pups had climbed over each other to reach the engorged teats and were suckling contentedly. Their mother was tired, but her breathing had settled, her temperature was fine and she looked remarkably peaceful with her pups nestling close to her. I reached down, lifted one up, and cuddled him, as he curled his little body around as if trying to touch his nose with his tail. The tail wagged furiously as a tiny pink tongue licked my hand and his mother thrashed her tail in harmony. I looked into those once doleful eyes and saw something new. I fancied it was pride.

Tariq popped in three times during that day. Each time he lingered, as if unable to leave. It was the emotion of the wedding, he protested. It was to check I was all right.

★ ☽ ★

The wedding hall hummed and palpitated. Fantasy trees bore neon fruit. Stuffed tigers and peacocks peeked from beneath plastic bushes, fairy lights flashed. Doors with heart-shaped windows leaked heady squeals.

We took our seats and the proceedings began. '*Asta boro, mahe man asta boro,*' 'walk slowly, my light of the night, go slowly,' they sang, as Maryam stepped serenely and gradually. Beside her Zaki looked uncomfortable in the spotlight. He lifted his chin, straightened his back and smiled. He was ready for her now and he was ready for happiness.

Sohaila billowed in a shimmering silk gown. Even Ahmed looked smart. He straightened his braces with studied concentration. It would be a terrible disgrace were his trousers to fall down.

The formalities washed over me. My impressions were

of a ceremony of symbols in which one wrong step promised certain misfortune. An arch of flowers, two thrones on a dais, and a table whose cloth was embroidered with gold and had been passed from mother to daughter over the generations. There were mirrors for fate, candles for happiness, herbs and spices to break spells, eggs for fertility, and pomegranates for joy. Platters held angelica, poppy and nigella seeds, salt to blind the evil eye, frankincense to burn it, baskets of painted eggs, walnuts and almonds. On one tray was henna, a shawl, a mirror wrapped in damask, a pudding with honey to sweeten the match, a Qur'an for good luck. They were sure to have need of it.

The ceremony was over. A sigh swept the crowd. Everyone began clapping. Eyes filled with tears, cheeks became rosy with emotion. Caps fluttered. Arms became tired with hugging, brows shiny with excitement. Friends smiled and waved. Relatives rushed to the dais to congratulate the newly-weds.

We feasted like kings. There was stuffed chicken, *ashak*, and aubergines with yoghurt and spinach. Dishes were piled high with mutton korma, with kebabs, and *pilau* rice jewelled with strips of carrot and raisins, almonds and pistachios, with chunks of lamb buried in it. The puddings were a luxury: a jelly, and *firni*, a sort of milk custard made with rice flour, and *abreyshum kabab*, all washed down with copious quantities of fizzy pop, lemonade and fake Coca-Cola from Pakistan, and a salty pink tea topped with clotted cream.

Afterwards came the dancing, the men with the men and the women with the women. Everyone knew the moves of the *atan*. Everyone moved shyly at first, leaning to the centre to clap on the beat, circling in a clockwise direction, then increasingly with abandon, clicking their fingers, wiggling, swirling, and stomping, blood throbbing with abandonment as a hundred pairs of bare feet shuffled in the dust. Sohaila, who counted herself among them, wiped beads of sweat from her forehead before they could mingle into rivers with the black kohl. She kissed her daughter with pride. How beautiful Maryam looked and how well she conducted herself. She was no longer a girl, but a woman.

In the men's area old men, baggy-trousered with white beards and cloth caps, squatted and sat together. The verdict was unanimous. A better outcome could not have been imagined. It was a most favourable and fortunate marriage; at last Allah had blessed them.

In the woman's area it was the past that dominated. The ladies reminisced, about good times and bad, victory and defeat, their faces heavy with joy and sorrow. Children gathered round to hear the love story of Prince Saiful Maluk and Jamal, his fairy princess. They were famous lovers in these parts.

The crowds dwindled. Snoring was emanating from a bush, and cicadas chirruped in chorus. Sohaila sang huskily and rhythmically. As the melody reached a high note her voice broke movingly. 'Bride, do not bow your head and cry bitter tears, This is God's wish, thanks be to God. Muhammad, God's messenger, solve her problems, make hard times easy . . .' I hoped it would come true, for all their sakes.

The wind stirred the dust from the cypresses, and a few muffled chords hung on its waves, as if the branches

CHAPTER 26

'Patience is Bitter, but its Fruit is Sweet'

صبر تلخ است و بهشیرین دارد .

I was going home in ten days' time. There was nothing more I could do here now. I had served my purpose and, by some miracle, I had survived. Zaki and Maryam were settled, Little Wolf was doing well, and the puppies were growing, scrambling, bouncing, rolling and peeing everywhere but on the newspaper I laid down for the purpose. Soon it would be Ramadan, and I wanted to get home before it began. I was homesick.

What to do about all the dogs was a question I had so far found impossible to answer. I had seen this coming, and had been dreading it. Taking them with me would mean a long period of quarantine, their separation from everything familiar. It was a cruelty I felt unable to inflict on them. However unbearable the thought of leaving them, I had to conclude that was in their best interests, but when the family offered to take them in, I still had mixed feelings. Little Wolf was a wild dog who would suffer no master.

'It's a big responsibility,' said Tariq. 'We shall have to do a lot of *thinking*.' He picked up a stick, Little Wolf seized the other end of it, and in a flash a tug of war began raging. They grumbled and growled in concentration, and it was some minutes later that we came up with a solution. I would set up a fund that gave Tariq a small income with which to buy ample quantities of meat and water. If Little Wolf disappeared again, the meat would go to the zoo. I should not be concerned, he said; there was no way he would see the little ones starve.

As I looked into his eyes I knew it was the right decision. Some might have wondered if I was too trusting, but as he fished out Ismael's Qur'an from his pocket, unwrapped it from its cloth and swore an oath on it, no one could have doubted him.

★ ☽ ★

As I walked down the street I didn't care that my headscarf was strangling me and I hardly noticed my shoes pinching. The puppies had been chewing them and the toes were all twisted, the soles were so thin I could feel the ground beneath my step. I was lucky to have shoes at all. I would never again take them for granted.

It was quarter past ten by the time I arrived. The children were standing in a row, lining up to wash their hands. There was no running water, but Maryam was measuring some out from a plastic container, rubbing little fingers, then inspecting them.

'Would anyone like to go first?' asked the teacher.

One little boy put his hand up tentatively, hair spiky with dirt, his torn anorak too big and his flies undone. A hushed silence fell, as bravely he walked to the front. 'There is no God but Allah, and the Prophet Muhammad is his messenger . . .' he began, with such a loud voice that the girls at the back put their hands over their ears. At just six years old he knew the words of the *Shahada* off by heart. He'd heard them, after all, at the moment of his birth when his father whispered them gently into his ear to prepare him for his destiny in this world. The boy grinned a gappy grin and sat back down. A little girl was tugging at Maryam's veil.

'Do you want to have a go, Emad?' said the teacher softly.

'Is Allah listening?' asked the little one.

'Of course he is!' said the teacher.

'Where is he, then?' blurted out another little boy.

'He is everywhere!' said Maryam, waving her arms in an expansive gesture.

'How come you have never seen him, then?'

'Because he is *invisible*!'

The children gazed at her in wonderment. The little girl began reading, and as she faltered over the words, her face went white against her dark flowery tunic. Soap was a luxury and the children often wore patterned clothes so the stains didn't show as much. 'God shows . . . the way . . . to . . . the truth.'

Silence descended. She returned to her seat, and a big clap resounded.

There was just enough time to practise the *Fatiha,* the opening of the Qur'an. 'In the name of Allah, Most Gracious, Most Merciful: Praise be to Allah, the Cherisher and Sustainer of the worlds. Most Gracious, Most Merciful . . .' The children's high voices chimed as one, the words flowing like poetry. It was said that someone who recited the Qur'an conferred a blessing on the listener. Allah would look after them.

'That was very beautiful,' I said from the back, and their faces shone with happiness. The bell rang and the children skipped off.

Maryam turned to me and smiled a knowing smile. Was marriage to Zaki the cause of her sparkling eyes, her rosy cheeks and the smile writ large across her beautiful face?

'How was the wedding night?' was a question I hardly dared to ask her. I need not have been anxious, for she volunteered the answer willingly – how their eyes had met in trepidation; how when he saw hers filled with fear and confusion, he had taken her hand. After several minutes of flirtation they had gone up to their room. That night, understanding her fear, he had not forced himself on her. They had spent time talking and laughing, and eventually he had planted a first soft kiss on her lips. She had given herself up to it, and despite all the briefings from her mother, the anxiety she had felt previously had melted away.

At first Zaki had seemed remote, detached, still with violent mood-swings. The depression turned outwards at times, making him petulant. Sometimes he flew off the handle without warning; but as she continued her support it was not long before he had let down his barriers. They were a natural consequence of all he had been through. It taught her patience. Already she had begun to see Zaki's good side revealed, glimpsed in his treatment of those around him, especially the children. He had become convinced that his suffering had happened for a purpose.

Without the experience of the kidnap, he would never have been able to experience such joy, for such heights of emotion could never have been realised without the depths. The ordeal had granted the reunion more meaning, and they appreciated each other in a way they would never otherwise have been able to do. How could you embrace such happiness had you not known such pain?

Having expected marriage to be a dull, dutiful affair, Maryam for her part was forced to admit that men, even Afghan ones, were not all the same. She was normally a composed and steady person who considered every step a thousand times before taking it, but the whole experience of marriage left her spiralling out of control in a good way. No one had been more surprised than she was when feelings began burning, like a fountain of fire. There was something about him that made her want to tell him everything. She even loved his big, hooked nose. She felt accepted, coming ever closer in her attachment to him. At times the sense of where she ended and he began faded at the edges. The oppositions of you and me, yours and mine, began to blend seamlessly as we. The differences of opinion cast shadows, but the light that blazed from the common ground was on fire. She was in love.

We said our goodbyes, and arranged to meet later. I walked into the sunshine and skipped. At last the darkness had been banished, and nothing could bring it back again.

CHAPTER 27

'Blood Cannot be Washed Out with Blood'

خون با خون شسته نمی شود .

The thud of dough against the walls of the bakery oven, the wail of prayer and the buzz of a helicopter. Those were the sounds at sunrise the morning of 1 October 2006. Light gleamed on the mud, radiating from the walls as if to transform them, as if the mud itself were gold.

I made my way to Shahr-e Nau street. There had been a pile of letters waiting for me at the post office, most sent long ago from my family advising me to return to England. There was another from Ismael inviting me to become his Sufi pupil and a raft from friends telling me I was mad.

One cut to the chase. 'Never forget', it said, 'the elbow is the strongest point on your body. If a robber asks for your wallet do not hand it to him, throw it on to the ground. If you are ever thrown in the trunk of a car, kick out the back lights, stick your arm through the hole and wave like fury. If someone has a gun, run. They will only hit a running target four in a hundred times, and even then they will probably miss your vital organs.' I wished I'd received that one earlier.

There were several lavender envelopes that day, one more recent than the others. I tore it open and skimmed the pages. Five blue sheets in neat copperplate, densely written on both sides. I glanced at a page at random, then looked away. I turned back a page to where blots of ink seeped and looked at that bit, staring in a daze as the paper slipped between my fingers. Only in those few sentences did the subject crop up. My father was in hospital again, wrote my mother. He was on a morphine drip. I was not to worry; there was nothing I could do. He had only weeks to live.

I walked purposefully on, distracting myself with the walls that curved and twisted, trailing my fingers in the bullet-shaped holes that pitted the surface in machine-gun patterns. I had to get home. I had to thank him, for his wisdom, for his friendship, simply for being a father.

We were gathering at the book shop in Shir Ali Khan. Genghis was driving, and Maryam was walking. From there it would be just a short distance to the *chaikhana*, the teahouse, and from then we would go on to the school to deliver some gifts: not many, just some blankets, games, clothes, and sweets. A moment of reckless optimism struck as I glanced at my watch. It was quarter to eight. The Annar Travel Bureau was not that far away, and if I was quick I could buy my plane ticket and still be in time for them.

'Where's my chocolate, missus?' As a little girl tugged at my sleeve, I bent down and talked to her.

'How old are you?' I asked her.

'I don't know,' she said. 'Can I have your pen?' She was still trailing behind me as I turned the corner.

I was just three streets away when the thud came from behind me, without warning. The ground trembled like the skin of a drum, my legs buckled, and my bones hit the ground with such force that for a second I thought I'd been shot. Ears ringing, I scrambled up on to my knees, squinting at the corona of fiery smoke and earth that stained the sky. The shouting was distant at first, then it came closer, in a cacophony of foreign words, screams, and wailing. Like a sleepwalker I staggered forward, and in that split second I decided to go back towards the blast.

I approached as the horror was unfolding. Shattered fragments began to take shape: the scorched carcass of a car; a pointed structure twisted; metal shards swaying in the wind like snakes; a textbook flung open, papers raining like feathers; windows shattered and tables smashed; a military vehicle in pieces; tree branches blown across the road; a tangle of prayer hats, shoes, arms, legs, a foot; pieces of flesh too horrific to describe. Turbaned men and blue-uniformed policemen, lungs choked with the dust and eyes blinded by it, were shouting.

Some brought cloths to cover the dead, others lifted the injured.

People were screaming in pain. A man cried out to me, his head streaming with blood. I took my scarf and wrapped it gently around it. Women were lying in the street, contorted. Those without hope we tried to cover. Then suddenly, the face of an angel, untouched. One of the men gathered the girl, cradling her gently, singing quietly, as if it might help. But then someone took her body from him, speaking words I did not understand.

I sank down into the dirt and took a long breath

through my narrowing lungs. A figure, stumbling, was speaking: 'Are you hurt?' I babbled something back, then it all went black.

When I opened my eyes again, a haze of dust was hovering. My chest felt heavy and my limbs seemed to tingle. I thought I saw the shadow of a man sitting silhouetted against the light, a mirage of a person. In my confusion I thought it was my father, but only when the dust had settled slightly did the image crystallise. I might not have recognised him, had it not been for the sweet scent wafting as he leant closer, all rosewater and musk. It was Genghis, of course.

We made our way slowly back to the bakery flat, and when my legs almost gave way I had a feeling he might have carried me. Genghis fed the dogs, and sat in the corner in silent vigil for what seemed like a very long while, so quiet that I barely noticed the door closing behind him. Maybe he thought I hadn't heard him when he had told me, and I wished that I hadn't. It had been some time before the dark crater relinquished the last of the dead, he said, and when finally they had taken Maryam's body away it had been light as a feather.

★ ☽ ★

It was a few more days before I fully took in what had happened. Kites still fluttered in the evening sky, dancing from the rooftops as they always had done, but no matter how hard the wind whistled it couldn't blow away the pain. The family bore their sorrow with such fortitude you might have been tricked into believing they had put it behind them. It was that killer Afghan pride again.

Genghis visited me often during the next few days. Tariq came with him once and sat silently watching the puppies. An affectionate lick from a tiny tongue and he almost smiled, before he remembered again. We talked, of the weather, of England, of anything but Maryam. It was just too raw. We stared at our plates of rice as if they were an enemy to be defeated. Twelve other lives had been lost that day, he said, and forty-two people had been injured, but he thought the child who had run after me had survived. Had she not done so, she would probably have died too. I think he said it to make me feel better.

The officials remained cagey as to the target, and whatever it had been wasn't important. It was an ordinary day in Kabul, just another attack on innocents. When a few days later the Taliban claimed responsibility for the incident, I didn't want to hear their excuses or understand their arguments. I felt filled with the absence of Maryam. I felt only the sense of being torn, of confusion and uncertainty. I was tired, I was angry, and I had had enough.

CHAPTER 28

'If the Forest Catches Fire, both Dry and Wet will Burn'

دربن خشک ترهم سوزر

A week had passed since the blast. A brooding hung in the air, as if the whole country had entered hibernation. Ramadan had brought a dullness to things. The mud of the buildings seemed lacklustre, the temperature of the air felt neither hot nor cold. Fathers and brothers, mothers and sisters ceased to eat. It was said that while fasting a person avoided sin and evil thoughts, forgave others theirs, and tamed their own passions. The observance of the fast was supposed to be a blessing rather than a time of trial; about remembering to take nothing for granted; removing daily distractions so the mind could focus on closeness with Allah. It was a special time that brought believers back to the heart of things. But no one needed reminding. How could they forget?

The sea of taxis and bicycles had dwindled. In the velvet dusk the wings of doves cut the air like a thousand tiny sabres, their gentle fluttering loud in the silence. The flock moved towards a desolate slope, grey against the deepening gold of the horizon, to where green flags marked the spots where the martyrs were buried. A few solitary mourners prayed nearby, crouching in the washed-out land.

In the late sun one boy carried a bucket and asked the mourners if, for a small fee, they would like him to wash the graves of their loved ones. I could have a single rose or, for a few extra *afghanis*, a small bunch tied with string. I bought two bunches, and watched the blood-red petals as they bathed in the golden light. Sohaila was standing some distance away at the graveside, but we could still tell she was crying because the arc of her body silhouetted against the sun was shaking. Zaki stood beside her, and in the stillness I felt the bond between them. Tariq and I were silent, because there were no words.

The boy appeared again. Would we like a prayer to remind us of our loved one, he asked matter-of-factly. We didn't need reminding. How could we forget? But Sohaila nodded all the same. The boy squatted, closed his eyes and recited a prayer from the Qur'an; and as he did so a bird hopped on the grave. 'She is in paradise,' he said solemnly. 'If she were in hell, it would have been a fly.'

Zaki took the photograph he had been holding and put it away into his pocket, as if it was too much to bear. Once he had drawn strength and hope from that picture, from the sweet smile, the kind, innocent eyes; but no longer. He had to keep it, he said, to remind him, but at the same time it represented everything now lost to him.

The wind stirred, lifting the little specks of birds struggling against the rising currents, and as the sun went down it felt as if it would never rise again. At the house, Ahmed recited the prayer for the dead in a hoarse voice.

The Afghans wept together, prayed together, grieved together. They shared their pain as they had always done, only this time I shared it with them. Afterwards we sat silently, cross-legged, for a while, as if there were no barriers between us. At first Zaki said little, swaying and rocking as if the movement might make it better. 'Maryam's dead, Maryam's dead,' he said once, as if reminding himself she had really gone. As he closed his eyes he could swear he could see in the darkness her face, her smile – the smile that brought light, he said, with his own sad smile.

In the kitchen, the gaslight penetrated the gloom, the smoke from the fire strong, the steam from the pans swirling in the dimness. The fire in the hearth tried to take the edge off the chill, but it was still cold. The women of the families had gathered, chopping vegetables and meat, searching for tiny stones in the rice, struggling with the great *dayg* pan, lifting hot coals from the lid and turning the mixture.

Sohaila cooked to be busy, to take her mind off things, but there was one recipe she was missing, the one for life. She picked up her youngest, embracing him fiercely with the force of the suffering inside her, blinking through her tears, snorting them up her nose as she talked. She remembered the moment she had first learned she was pregnant with Maryam, consumed by an intense longing to hear herself called a mother. She would say soft things to the child in her belly, reassuring it, bathing it in love, promising to look after it. Of course, when she had first learnt she had given birth to a girl, she had been disappointed. She felt upset and terrified. But everything had changed when she saw her, this tiny person with magic eyes. She could tell then what joy and happiness the child would give her. It was as if all her family and her husband's family were in the little girl.

As a child Maryam had been playful, diligent, spirited. She had a range of body signals – a well-timed sigh, an imploring gaze, and, when she was older, an upward roll of the eye. Every day they had sat together at the kitchen table, Maryam peeling the potatoes, passing them to her mother to chop. The two of them were always together, often silent, often talking or praying together, at night falling asleep together. Tariq had been a good boy, too, but he had spent most of the time with his father, selling photographs he had taken, or playing with his friends. Now life had robbed her of that joy and had replaced it with emptiness. A mother should never have to witness the death of her child.

Some time later Tariq drove me home, full of tears he would not let fall. He had his own way of dealing with things, he said. He would try to recall scenes from their childhood together, happy memories. They played over and over in his head, journeys of the mind, to Paghman and Istalif, to the lake at Qargha, places that reminded him of when they were young, when they would fly their kites and climb mulberry trees.

That night I was filled with the pain of the others, too numb to feel my own. I puffed out the candle and was aware of moths flapping, though there was no light for them to circle. Maryam had been right. Allah was invisible, all right. He was invisible because he was absent.

CHAPTER 29

'One Day You See a Friend, the Next a Brother'

یک روز دیدی دوست روز دیگر برادر

Goodbyes had never been my strong point, and when the time came I would rather have crept off secretly, but no one would have any of it. I took one last look around my room and ran my fingers over the carving of the door, admiring the workmanship. I was filled with sorrow to leave this place. I had grown used to it. Little Wolf was in no doubt that something was up. As she cocked her head questioningly, I was at a loss how to explain to her that I was leaving.

Genghis carried my rucksack downstairs. Outside the bakery the rancid stench mingled with the rising dough in a sweet-and-sour effect. I hardly noticed the trickle of urine that had leaked from the drain in the centre of the path, and which was running over my shoe. One of the boys popped his head out of the bakery and shouted 'Come into my oven!', reaching into the furnace with a shovel and extracting the *naan*, as another boy was folding it. They smiled at me, faces glowing like street-sellers' charcoal burners. The baker looked sad to see me go, and

I couldn't help wondering if it had something to do with the rent he was losing. But as I handed him the great yellow key, inviting him to visit me in England, he beamed a smile that seemed genuine. He had been tempted to pass on my details to the police, he said, but he was glad he hadn't. He'd have made more money that way, though.

The taxi had had an overhaul to make it dog-friendly. What Omar really meant by that was that he had had put a blanket on the back seat. 'Next time,' he said cheerily, as he lifted my bags in, 'I will give you a full guided tour of the country.'

'I'll take you up on that one day,' I said.

'When peace returns, *Inshallah*,' he bowed.

'*Inshallah*,' we all echoed.

Omar drove as if there might have been eggs on the bonnet, which was just as well as the traffic was crawling so he couldn't go fast anyway. We were jammed in to bursting point, Tariq in the back with Genghis and Little Wolf, while I squeezed in the front with a box full of dogs on my lap. It was a typical Afghan crush, said Genghis, who was taking up most of the room himself.

At the door of the house the children were waiting. Wide eyes in small faces peered beneath the blanket in the large cardboard box, which was full of equally wide eyes in even smaller faces. Both sets of eyes blinked, and there were yelps of excitement all round.

I picked up the puppies one by one and kissed them farewell, and their mother turned her head, looking at me as though she knew what was happening. I threw my arms around her neck, and still the dog did not flinch. How far she had come, the little wolf that had been wild and scared. 'You are a mother now,' I whispered, 'you must be strong.' Whereas I had often struggled to grasp the various tail-waggings, the sniffings and snufflings, the pricking up of the ears, it had frequently seemed that the dog in her own way had understood everything. But what had never been in any doubt were the many words Little Wolf expressed with her eyes. And it was with those eyes that she spoke to me now, for it seemed as if she knew I would understand the one eye-word she was saving for me. That word was love.

Tears slipped down my cheeks as the dog spoke it now, loud and clear, and though I tried to wipe them it was no use. Gently nuzzling my knee, the dog said the word, over and over. 'I'll see you again,' I told her. It was a promise that would never be broken.

She looked at me questioningly, sat up straight and took to her heels, running around wildly, as if something were chasing her. Again she did it and again, three times in all. It was an ancient way that dogs had of saying goodbye, said Sohaila, hugging me tightly.

Ahmed made a long, deep bow, wiping his face on the tail of his turban. He was pleased to see his prayers had been working. There was still a small flicker of hope for my soul. '*Dushmane daanaa behtar az dost-e nadan,*' he said. It meant a wise outsider was better than a stupid insider.

★ ☽ ★

At the airport I turned to the men I owed my life to, at a loss as to what to say to them.

Genghis's beard was bristling with emotion.

'It was a rather dark journey, wasn't it . . .' I said.

He shook his head pensively. *'Na burda ranj ganj muiasar namishawad.'* It was only when it was dark enough that you could see the stars, he said.

Tariq looked down, unable to meet my gaze. He lifted his eyes, tousled his hair, clasped my hands in his a little too long, let them go, then put his right hand on his chest. It was reaching from his heart to mine. It showed he meant it.

'That journey doesn't end here.'

'It is just the beginning,' I smiled.

'*Zenda bashi,*' he said, 'be alive!'

I walked away and did not look back, for I could not. Mutual incomprehension had become trust. Today we understood each other perfectly.

CHAPTER 30

'In a Ditch where Water has Flowed, it will Flow Again'

آسِ مَّر ٔ پارٔ آمٔ ٔ ٔ ٔ ہوگا

London was grey and cold, the airport full of strangers with pale faces. The taxi-driver said nothing except, 'You look tired, love.' He was absolutely right, he just didn't know how tired.

As I turned the key in the lock, my front door opened reluctantly, as a mountain of cards and letters behind it gave way. I took one from the top and peeled it open, and as the card slid out from the envelope, the words on it stared at me blankly: *In Sympathy*. My fingers let it slip and I watched it floating to the floor, almost oblivious of the high-pitched screech from the answer-phone. I pulled out the plug and let it die. I couldn't think straight.

I walked into the bathroom, numb with shock. I turned on the tap, tipped in the bath milk and frothed it, then lay under a carpet of bubbles in the hot water until my prune-like fingers and toes could wrinkle no further. It had been so long since I had a proper bath, but I wasn't really enjoying it. I stood up and dried myself mechanically, hardly noticing the softness of the towel I should have been luxuriating in, and lathered myself with an array of potions, all promising to turn the clock back. It was too late. I barely recognised the worn features looking back at me in the mirror. How old I had grown.

The knock on the door was almost inaudible. I opened it and forced a smile, and my mother forced one back. She looked small in her emerald coat, her face lost in the huge collar. Her hair, always the colour of an autumn leaf, had taken on a frosty tinge, and her bird-like frame seemed to have shrunk further. As my arms filled with her slender bones, it felt for a moment as if we were going to crush each other, and as she kissed my cheek it was a kiss born of shared tears.

'Why didn't you tell me?' I said.

'I didn't want to tell you on the phone.' she replied, 'It would have been an awful conversation. Why didn't you tell me about the attack in Kabul?'

I looked at her and as our eyes met we both knew. We had just been trying to protect one another.

The next few weeks passed uneventfully. My mother came to stay and we cooked together, pies, casseroles, roasts we couldn't eat. Maybe in time it would get better; maybe, if we could just somehow keep going, we might see past the loss, and get better at distracting ourselves. We found comfort in the kind words of others who had lost loved ones, and who maintained that the heart was the strongest muscle of the body; that no matter how much damage it suffered it would always repair itself. We talked more than we had ever done, of the past, of blessings yet to come, of happiness almost realised. I remembered the piercing outward wail of an Afghan mother, against the silent, stifled inward wail of my own, not knowing which was worse. There was nothing like a mother's love, as intense, as awe-filled, and as brilliant.

Friends welcomed me home, and I was grateful to see them again, but when it came to explaining it was hard to know where to start. When I did try, I failed miserably, and met with flummoxed expressions. I didn't know what to say to them. I bumped into one of my old professors, who said very little, except that he thought I might try Egypt next time; the architecture was fascinating.

Portobello Market hummed and buzzed as it had always done, but there was something missing. It was Mr Noor, who, it turned out, was often away these days or at mosque, and had charged much of the daily running of the business to his sons and nephews. As I began my story their lips twisted.

'Who is Tariq?' they asked with baffled expressions. They had never heard of him.

'A great man,' I said.

'And this Genghis person – what sort of man was he?'

'A warrior.'

★ ☽ ★

Autumn gave up its amber leaves. The air became fresh, crisped by a chill wind as we headed up north to my mother's cottage. It had been so long since I was last there that I had almost forgotten its beauty, the weathered sandstone walls, the tall, uneven windows.

A little later we closed the gate behind us, wandering past hedgerows, over a footbridge spanning a reedy stream where soundlessly the water flowed. On the horizon the mountains were steely grey, and the end of autumn had drained the landscape of its colour, with only an occasional patch of brown against the bleached expanse where a tractor had been working.

At the base of the valley the fells parted, and the land fanned out into a wash of pale shades: the gold of the stubble, dark smudges of woods, mottled browns and greens. Beyond the windy path a canopy of oaks and birches and a cherry tree shaded a small patch where the earth was freshly turned.

'He was so proud of you,' said my mother, as we lingered beside the grave.

'He never said.'

'He tried to tell you in his own way . . .'

'I know,' I said, taking my mother's hand and squeezing it.

I lifted my face to the sky, allowing the wind to dry the strands of hair clinging to my cheek.

A flock of birds swooped overhead, I watched their blue-grey undersides flashing white as they turned against the land, thinking of Maryam, of her strength and her spirit, of the things that connected us rather than those which drew us apart.

We lingered a while longer by the grave in a silence that both drew us together and brought us apart from everything; and somehow, in the absence of speaking, we found a separate peace where only we belonged.

It was much later that the tears finally fell, when I was alone, and when it was raining so hard no one could have told the difference in the wetness on my face. When they did fall they ran in rivers like the memories that flooded my senses. Through the blur of my vision, finally I saw something with clarity. It was the realm of all I did not know, the realm of my ignorance.

Only now did it feel as if I was beginning to mourn. Loss had shown me that all lives are precious, and for that I would always be grateful. It had taught me how to treasure my own relationships and every precious moment they gave. In life as in war, you were bound to lose those you loved, whichever side you were on, whatever your cause. You would always suffer, but in that suffering you faced a choice. You could shed tears because they were lost to you, or you could smile because they had lived. You could live for yesterday, or you could be glad for tomorrow because of yesterday. You could turn inwards, or you could do what they would have wanted you to do – smile, love and go on.

Hope endured always, because it was the cracks of a broken heart that let the light in. In the end, love eclipsed everything, because it was stronger and brighter than death.

Epilogue

It was four a.m. I had been dreaming of a zoo with empty cages. The animals had mutinied, and I was rushing round with a chair trying to find them all to shoo them back in. I was wide awake when the phone rang, worrying about the animals in Kabul. I picked up the receiver.

War was waging even more fiercely in the south, said Tariq. He did not expect it would end. Genghis had left his sheep to graze, and was last seen heading off to Helmand where he had enlisted in the army. He still refused to accept any payment for helping find Zaki. It was his honour, he said. Dostum was still ruling the north of Afghanistan, and was backing Karzai because Karzai had promised him autonomy. His friend, the Mullah, was still teaching the message of the Qur'an. He was apparently delighted with the blue tablets I had sent him.

Little Wolf was doing well. She would disappear often, sometimes for days, sometimes longer, but by now they had all quite got used to her comings and goings. It would have been wrong to try to pin her down. He fancied she might have returned to the bakery to where she knew there was food and water, and where she might have thought I was still living, though he could not be sure of it. In any case, she always came back eventually.

The puppies were thriving, he said. Though Ahmed had objected at first, Sohaila had insisted on keeping them, at least until they found good homes for them. They were wild creatures, and very smelly. None of them responded to any commands. Kittens would have been much cleaner.

Having said that, the puppies had a charisma of their own: they were shy and timid like their mother, but equally spirited. One in particular, the smallest, was a real character. He was wary of men but with lady dogs he was all charm, swaggering round them, tail held high. They were hoping Ismael might take him, together with his Qur'an that Tariq was taking to Herat to return to him. Although the idea of an attachment might have been out of keeping with his Sufi spirit of freedom, it would be educational for both of them.

Events had moved on since I had left Afghanistan. He thought Kaftar's son had been murdered. Keen to avenge his death, Kaftar had set out to track down the perpetrators and had sought the help of many influential men in Afghanistan, not just Dostum. When all else had failed, it was said she had killed the murderer with her bare hands, and had been captured by the authorities. Naturally she fiercely denied any involvement in the matter. The Guantanamo prisoner who had led us to the kidnappers had been re-recruited by the Taliban. The animals at the zoo were being fed, albeit sporadically, and Tariq was doing what he could to deliver extra supplies. He had booked his flight to Mecca and it was going to be the journey of a lifetime; it was nice of me to buy it for him. Would I be able to help him buy a wife, too?

Zaki was keeping up appearances, he said, but there was an emptiness about him, as if his very soul had been drained, because the petals had fallen. He spent days in black depressions, but he was dealing with those, said Tariq, like everyone else in Afghanistan who had to deal with things. They were all part of the brotherhood of all who had known suffering, a brotherhood that held sisters also, burka or no burka. Sohaila was finding it hardest. Sometimes she would sing, like the nightingale's song for the love of a rose, but death had reached out and touched her too many times. It felt now as if she were mourning her own end. She would have given gladly up her own life if she could have, but in the end she could not save her daughter. They never would make sense of it, but they thanked God for the years they had known her.

There was a pause between us then, and a silence in reflection. Happiness was not a state of being, he thought, but a series of moments, transient, spontaneous, reached for and grasped. You never knew when joy would come into your life, and when it did, you should make the most of it. He hesitated again. He'd almost forgotten to mention that the Judas tree would be blossoming soon. He wished his sister could have seen it.

As I put down the phone I realised how deeply I missed my Afghan friends, their pervading good will that no war could destroy, their courage, and their dignity. I had been honoured by their friendship. They had restored my faith in the good intention of Islam, above all in the power of the human spirit to stay hopeful, despite everything life threw at it. I missed the country, too. I knew now why so many people loved it there. There was a hypnotic quality about it almost impossible to put into words, a sense of place that sucked you in. When it spat you out you felt empty, displaced.

Last but not least, I missed Little Wolf, the brave dog who had overcome her own fear and so had taught me much about my own. We had touched each other's lives at a time when we both needed it, and for that I would always be grateful. I realised now a truth which must console all those who have ever truly loved an animal: that those short episodes we were lucky enough to spend together did not have to mean emptiness after they ended, whether by death or by separation. The void could never be filled, but the memories would always live on. Although they appeared gone forever, they were never lost inside you.

I had set off to Afghanistan to find something, only to lose something, someone who had been dear to me. I never found out who else had died in the Kabul blast, and even now I didn't want to know. Images from the square in London which had been buried in my mind now began to resurface. Memories stirred in me as I thought of it. Flashes of moments forgotten and buried didn't make what happened in Kabul any clearer, but the two attacks connected in my memory, like terrifying jigsaws of the same scene. Though the individual pieces were quite different, the whole seemed to fit together. It was a picture of senseless-ness, of pointless sacrifice and the futility of a war that could never be won.

There were many different cancers – poverty, revenge, anger – cancers that ate at the soul rather than the body. Some would have said terrorism was the worst of all of them. The name of Islam would always be hijacked to justify actions that were unjustifiable. In the end those who chose guns and bombs to make their point were waging war not against Western values, nor Christianity, nor our governments. Ultimately their war was one against peace itself.

The questions that had dogged me at the outset of my journey felt just as illusory as they had ever done, but at the end of it all I hoped that, if nothing else, my own experience had taught me to understand them more deeply. The answers lay deep and were rooted in history. The rifts would take many years to heal and maybe they never would. Perhaps a starting point for resolution lay in the Qur'an itself, the book that decreed: 'Goodness and evil cannot be equal. Repay evil with what is better; then he who was your enemy will become your friend.' Above all, said the Qur'an about your enemies: 'If they seek peace, then you seek peace. And trust in God, for He is the One that hears and knows all things.' I hoped that some day our leaders would call on all those who named themselves our enemies to meet, to fight like men with reasoned argument. If they valued the word of God in their own holy book, they would have a duty to respond.

For my own part I was lucky. I had wandered in amongst the shadows and, by some miracle, had survived to tell the tale. In the terra incognita of myself I had travelled from the head and ended up at the heart. I had felt imprisoned by something and had been released from it. Above all, I had found love, trust and friendship, and in so doing had reached the crux of what Islam meant to me personally in a way that was real and that allowed me to find my own peace with it, and with God.

I went out and stood on the balcony, blinking across the rooftops, carving with my gaze a path of light through darker and deeper shadows. As I watched, I saw the darkness was, in fact, not black, but blue, swirled by the wind into patches of lilac, grey and purple, where a few stars burst out.

An electric storm was breaking. Hypnotised by the forks of lightning as they flashed across the horizon, it occurred to me how the light and the dark were not opposites after all. They were linked. Lives formed patterns of sun and shade. Some made perfect circles, whereas others took shape in ways we would never understand.

We were all part of an unpredictable ballet, at once daunting, painful, and luminous. Life was a slow process, a gradual dawning of realisation, a metamorphosis during which the spirit was moulded by a process of breaking and regrouping in a baffling synchronicity. We were moving to the tune of our own strange music, fragile and tumultuous. Steps uncertain at the time could often only be mastered in hindsight. Sometimes we would swap shoes and learn empathy with others. Great blows jolted the senses, while so often the breakages remained on the inside, grumbling beneath the surface until eventually, in the twinkling of an eye, finally they burst to the surface, allowing us to turn in our understanding, as if in pirouette.

The sky had settled. The moon yawned and the inky stillness gave itself to the light of dawn. The faint glow began in the east and a mist crept over the rooftops. Traffic headlights twinkled here and there as if to take over from the fading stars. Life wasn't about waiting for the storm to pass. It was about learning to dance with the rain and the darkness. In such harsh conditions, you were almost bound to slip and fall, but sometimes, just sometimes, if you were fast enough, and if you were lucky, that same darkness might twirl you into a night where moonbeams shone.

Acknowledgements

I am greatly indebted to the many friends and acquaintances who read the manuscript for this book and for their kind and perceptive comments, In particular I would like to thank Alex Mason, Mohammad Shaker Enayat, Dr Mohammad Najib Omari, Joseph Omidvaran, Michael Goldberg, Anthony Holden, Maureen Barrymore, Geoff Cowling, Helen Saberi, Simon Barb, Fiona Spencer-Thomas, Christopher Rundle, Alexander McCall Smith, Matthew Parris and Andrew Carmichael.

Denise Robertson has given kindness, time and patience in her reading of the various drafts. I am deeply in her debt for imparting to me some very useful advice on the art of writing. Special thanks are also due to editor extraordinaire Alan Brooke for his many wonderful editorial suggestions and comments; and to Prudence Fay for her careful reading of the text and useful recommendations. And Steve Crisp and Ian Hughes have made the book a beautiful object.

Professors Charles Melville and Gerald Hawting both helped to steer me in the right direction when I began writing the book, and provided invaluable advice as well as great coffee. I owe thanks also to my dear friend and teacher Sulafa Nashawati, to Thomas Stuttaford, Liz Dallas-Ross, Alan Jessop and to Lucy Bridges; and to my Persian teachers, Sorour Dundon, who taught me that trying to hold two watermelons in one hand was futile, but that holding one in each was an interesting way to try juggling; and Minoo Eskandari who showed me what an amazing language Farsi is, and that when learning it, patience is bitter but its fruit sweet.

Thanks are due to the boys, Benjamin de Rivaz, Captain Bertie Kerr and Captain Sam Burrell for their heroism and for sharing the reality of what it is like to be a soldier on the front line in Helmand. And I am grateful to Freshta Omer, Khatera Omer, Noor Noori and Nasir Saberi for their help and kindness with the printing and distributing of Little Books Afghanistan.

Haji Noor Ahmed helped to introduce me to those in Afghanistan who helped and protected me. I know that he has advised many who are living and working in Kabul or reporting from there and in so doing he has given all of us a considerable service.

Words fail me when it comes to expressing thanks to my Afghan friends but for whom the book would not have existed. I owe my life to Genghis, Tariq, Maryam, Sohaila and Ahmed. I will never forget their friendship, their kindness, their grace and their courage. Finally, I would like to thank my father, whose suffering opened my eyes to how life really is; and my mother, the best dancer I know, for forgiving all my wrong-footedness.